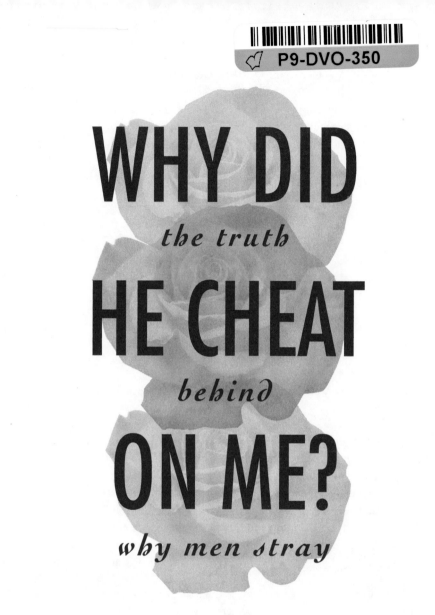

WHY DID

the truth

HE CHEAT

behind

ON ME?

why men stray

RONA SUBOTNIK, LMFT
Bestselling coauthor of *Surviving Infidelity*

Adamsmedia
Avon, Massachusetts

Published by Adams Media, a division of F+W Media, Inc.
57 Littlefield Street, Avon, MA 02322. U.S.A.
www.adamsmedia.com

ISBN 10: 1-4405-0054-1
ISBN 13: 978-1-4405-0054-1
eISBN 10: 1-4405-0713-9
eISBN 13: 978-1-4405-0713-7

Printed in the United States of America.

10   9   8   7   6   5   4   3   2   1

Library of Congress Cataloging-in-Publication Data
is available from the publisher.

This publication is designed to provide accurate and authoritative information with regard to the subject matter covered. It is sold with the understanding that the publisher is not engaged in rendering legal, accounting,
or other professional advice. If legal advice or other expert assistance is
required, the services of a competent professional person should be sought.
—From a *Declaration of Principles* jointly adopted by a
Committee of the American Bar Association and a Committee
of Publishers and Associations

Many of the designations used by manufacturers and sellers to distinguish
their product are claimed as trademarks. Where those designations appear
in this book and Adams Media was aware of a trademark claim, the designations have been printed with initial capital letters.

The stories in this book are based on real clients, but names and specifics
have been changed to protect identities.

This book is available at quantity discounts for bulk purchases.
For information, please call 1-800-289-0963.

To all the women who have experienced the heartbreak and despair of infidelity and with appreciation for all the women who have shared their stories with me. I hope all now enjoy a life of peace and well-being.

Contents

Acknowledgments

Dear Readers:

Writing a book is a complex process and there are many people who help you along the way. Their help is much appreciated. I want to especially thank my husband, Norman, who read this book chapter by chapter over and over again as I requested. He is an excellent proofreader, editor, and kind critic.

This book is so very much better because of his patience and willingness to reread one book so very many times. I particularly appreciate his cheerfully going along with so many dinners and lunches out or takeouts during "crunch time" as I worked on this book. Now that it is finished, I promise home-cooked meals and will not ask him to read another thing (until the next book, that is).

All of my family—Adrienne and Todd Sharp, Dr. Kenneth Subotnik and Dr. Stephanie Woo, and Debra and Mathew Tratt—have been supportive of me as I wrote. I am most appreciative of the insights shared by my daughter, Debra Tratt, who read many chapters and gave me encouraging feedback; and my daughter-in-law, Dr. Stephanie Woo, who read areas in her specialty of psychopathology, which she teaches at Pepperdine University. And much appreciation to my son Kenneth, who came to my rescue more than once when I was caught in one of my computer glitches.

My daughter, Adrienne Sharp, was cheering me along from the sidelines as she was meeting her own deadline on her next exciting novel.

I received encouragement and support from my friends, "The Therapy Sisters," who meet twice a month for lunch to catch up with each other and share and discuss professional news. They are Marriage and Family Therapists Marilyn Kaplan and Ceil Feldman; Anger Management Therapist Karen Golob; and Medical Hypnotherapist Dr. Lois K. Rubin. I particularly want to thank Lois, Karen, and Marilyn for reading the entire manuscript and sharing their insights with me. In addition, I appreciate the comments of my friend, psychologist Dr. Virginia A. Simpson, who specializes in bereavement counseling. I thank all of you for your friendship and your contributions to this book. I thank Peggy Vaughan for her never-failing support.

And last but really first of all, I want to thank those who are responsible for helping my thoughts to become this book. I want to thank my agent, Julie Castiglia, for our partnership of twenty years, for her support and for always having my interests at heart. Additionally, I want to thank Adams Media for our long partnership of twenty years and for having helped to make this book one that will be an important addition to their collection. Those at Adams who have been so expert in their help are Laura Daly and Kate Petrella. I especially thank Laura my editor, for her professionalism, expertise, and thoughtfulness and for making this book better with her suggested additions, and probing questions. I am grateful to my copyeditor Kate Petrella for her excellence and thoroughness as she reviewed this manuscript. This resulted in a much improved book. I would also like to thank the design department of Adams Media for their creativity in designing this cover and the book in such a way that I keep gazing at it in admiration and appreciation.

Finally, I want to thank the men and women, who, over the years, have shared their stories with me, wrote, e-mailed, and had telephone conferences with me. I appreciate your confidence in me, and I continue to wish you good luck as you resolve your issues from the tangled triangle of infidelity. I admire you all for coming forward for help. Best wishes to you.

Most sincerely,
Rona Subotnik

Introduction

This book will help you understand affairs, and by doing so find the answer to the question *Why Did He Cheat on Me?* Many women say that if her husband or partner ever had an affair, she would leave him. This would be a very simple non-thinking attempt at a solution to a very complex situation, and one that may backfire on her. When faced with infidelity, understanding it will probably help her realize that the answer is not simple. I believe in learning as much as you can about this issue before making a decision, and that is what this book is about.

The information you will find in *Why Did He Cheat on Me?* comes from what I have observed from working with many women and men over the past twenty-six years, and from the hundreds of support groups I have led. I also refer to the work and research of other authorities in the mental health field. I use literature, plays, TV shows, and films where it helps to illustrate a point. If I make a point from an actual person, I disguise names, locales, and individuals so that they would not be recognizable to anyone, including themselves. All confidences are honored. This book will be of interest to those in committed relationships as well as those who are married. I use the words *affair* and *infidelity* interchangeably and the terms *other woman*, *affair person*, and *affairee* interchangeably as well.

In **Part I, The Picture of an Affair,** you will learn the most important things to know about affairs. Perhaps the most important is that there are **six different kinds of affairs.** Four are the traditional type—an affair with touching—while the other two are nontraditional, **without** touching. The latter are just as threatening to a marriage as is the traditional affair. The type of affair your husband is having is critical for you to know and identify. Affairs are complex events in a person's life, because not all affairs are the same, people are different, and many people are involved. You will learn about the role played by previous family generations, and the effect on the next generation. Affairs go through stages, and each will be explained to you. You also will read about an interesting theory of love, one that is easy to understand and can be applied to infidelity.

In **Part II**, titled **What Causes Affairs?** you will learn the reasons that many have affairs, which exist on a *continuum* from the ones that are most easy to resolve to those that are the hardest to resolve. The first chapter starts with the stress of transitions, and the last chapter in this part describes the most difficult types of affairs to resolve, those involving men who have psychological and personality issues. As you can see, each section of the book is written so that you see the differences and you can locate the kind of affair you are dealing with and understand what it means to your future.

Part III is called **Restructuring the Marriage**. It puts together all the information provided to this point and gives you the answer to the question *Why Did He Cheat on Me?* It explains the emotional life of the wife and husband as they go through the disclosure of an affair. There is a chapter titled Coping Skills, which includes effective communication, dealing with anger, and ways to cope with the many uncomfortable emotions that are the aftermath of an affair.

Each chapter ends with an exercise designed to help you understand your situation more clearly. The exercise will be based on what you have already read in the book, applied to your situation.

My goal as a marriage and family therapist is to help people through the pain of dealing with infidelity, whether a couple visits me in my office or reads one of the books I have written. As I write, I have you in mind and earnestly hope that I have explained the issues and my concerns with the compassion I feel and the knowledge I have gained over the years.

You can visit my website by going to *www.surviveinfidelity.com* or *www.ronasubotnik.com*.

I wish you well along this journey. I am sure at the end you will know more than when you started, you will have many of your questions answered, and you will pick the road that's right for you. I send you my best wishes.

Turn the page, and let's begin our journey.

—Rona B. Subotnik, Licensed Marriage and Family Therapist

Part I

THE PICTURE OF AN AFFAIR

"I spent months learning to live with a single incidence of infidelity. And I would like to say that a single incidence is easy to overcome, but it is not."

RESILIENCE BY ELIZABETH EDWARDS

"This was a whole lot more than a simple affair. This was a love story. A forbidden one, a tragic one, but a love story at the end of the day."

MARK SANFORD, GOVERNOR OF SOUTH CAROLINA

chapter one

WHAT DOES AN AFFAIR LOOK LIKE?

Tim tries to be very quiet as he turns the lock on the front door of his house in Chevy Chase, Maryland. He takes off his shoes and tiptoes up the carpeted steps. He stops in little Timmy's room to kiss his son's face and affectionately pat his head, then goes to Rosie's room to view his daughter sound asleep. He nearly trips over the dolls on the floor. Tim smiles and thinks, "She must have been playing when her mother thought she was asleep." He picks up the dolls and tenderly kisses Rosie's chubby cheek. In the bedroom he shares with his wife, Molly, he tries to be very quiet, but Molly stirs and wakens. Tim tells her that his office meeting had gone on longer than expected. He promises himself once again that he will stop his affair with Laura, which has been going on for nearly a year. He slips into bed, gives Molly a kiss on her brow, and in a few minutes drifts off to sleep.

What makes a man cheat on his loved one? It is not always, as some think, because he is unhappy, or she is just impossible to live with. It is not always unhappy couples who experience an affair; happy couples can be touched by infidelity as well. Many factors contribute to the reason he cheats. We will sort out this complicated picture in the following pages.

What Is a Committed Relationship?

Before we begin, it's important to define the type of partnerships covered in this book: committed relationships. We will be looking at both men and women who have committed to each other, either in a marriage ceremony or by a verbal commitment.

The word *verbal* is crucial because it indicates that the commitment was intentional and agreed to by each person. The committed couple has **spoken** their promises to each other. Some couples speak these words privately, but others have their friends and family join them in a ceremony or ritual that honors the commitment they have made to one another. The expectations and promises of a committed couple are the same as for a married couple: They are thought of as a married couple, and many have bought a home together and have children together.

Committed relationships are not simply based, as many people think, on the amount of time a couple has been together. In fact, time together is *not* the indicator of a committed relationship. Other people, as well as the couple themselves, assume that because they have been together for so many years, a commitment must exist. Some women who have come to me for therapy have told me that when they asked for a commitment after being with their partner quite a long time, they were shocked to find the answer was "no." In many cases, these relationships ended at that point.

In this book, I use the term "marriage" to mean any *committed relationship* unless otherwise designated. I will use the terms "husband" and "wife" as well as "partner"; you can correspond these terms to whatever nomenclature is appropriate in your particular relationship.

What Is an Affair?

An affair is a maladaptive way to cope with issues that develop during the course of a committed relationship or marriage—issues that are not being resolved well, or that arise from problems that one or both of the individuals brings to the marriage or relationship. Sometimes people feel that marriage will solve their problems, but their problems may be too much for the marriage to accommodate. When I describe affairs and tell you about those involved, try to keep this definition in mind. I do not blame anyone; I try to understand everyone, and bring that knowledge to you.

"Not all affairs are the same" is a theme you will notice throughout this book. The cause of an affair can be as simple as poor communication or as complex as personality problems. Therefore, we will look at what the affair might be about, what problems there might be, and what can be done about the situation.

Understanding is another major theme that is emphasized in this book. If you understand why the affair happened, you are better able to address those underlying issues and perhaps prevent another affair from happening.

Degrees of Affairs Seen on a Continuum

There are four types of traditional affairs, which can best be understood by seeing them on a continuum according to the degree of emotional attachment or connectedness of the cheating partner to the affair person. The continuum starts at one end with the serial affair and ends with the long-term affair:

1. Serial affair
2. Fling
3. Romantic love affair
4. Long-term affair

Let's look at each of the four types and at four couples who are experiencing an affair in their marriage. You will begin to see how different affairs can be as you learn more about the types and the meaning of each.

Serial Affairs

A man having a serial affair has no emotional attachment to any of his partners in his affairs. This behavior can occur in real life or online. As the name indicates, his affairs come in a series, such as a series of one-night stands, or a series of short affairs. It can also be visits to prostitutes, or any combination of these. He may also have many affairs at one time. He can walk away from one affair only to start another soon after or even at the same time.

CHARACTERISTICS OF SERIAL AFFAIRS
- Series of one-night stands, many affairs of short duration, visits to prostitutes.
- He is not likely to seek therapy.
- He has no emotional connection to affair partner(s).
- He has no emotional connection to his marriage or commitment.
- He can walk away from the affair(s).
- He is not likely to marry the affair person.

The Long-Term Threat of the "Other Woman"
There is little threat to the marriage in terms of the husband leaving his wife for a woman with whom he has had one of these many

affairs. If he does leave, he is likely to soon start another series of sexual encounters. His affairs are a response to his own emotional issues. His infidelity may be a pervasive behavior that began in his young adult years, or it may be a new behavior.

What Is He Like?

He can fool many women, because he knows how to be very charming. A serial lover is a "risky" partner who is at risk for having a series of affairs because of his own emotional or psychological makeup. In looking back, it can sometimes be seen in his premarital behavior, including cheating on previous girlfriends, hanging out with guys who cheat, and thinking that treating women this way is "cool." He is unable to be faithful because of emotional issues that plague him. He does not necessarily stand out in any negative way; he may be your neighbor or a well-spoken businessman or a television personality. Please see Chapter 9 for more on men like this.

A FICTIONAL SERIAL AFFAIR

We can see serial lovers portrayed on television or in the movies. The character of Don Draper, played by Jon Hamm in the popular television program *Mad Men*, is an excellent example of a serial lover. He grew up as an abused child who left home as soon as he could. Don walled himself off from his past and had one affair after another. Don's wife confronted him with her suspicions, but he could not give up the affairs. His wife loved him and was the ideal wife of her era (the 1950s), but she could not meet his psychological needs. In fact, no woman could.

The paradox of the serial lover is that he can be charming and popular, and have many affairs, but cannot establish closeness with anyone. Though he is trying to control every aspect of his life with his many affairs, he is unlikely to find true happiness with anyone.

Lizzie and Larry

Lizzie was interrupted from working on her painting for an art show when the telephone rang. The voice was unfamiliar. "Hello, this is Susan. I'm having an affair with your husband. I thought we should meet." A chill ran through Lizzie's body. She knew immediately this was not a cruel joke. She hung up; she had received many such calls over the course of her fifteen-year marriage.

She was not shocked when she learned of Larry's latest affair, but she was heartbroken. It was not the first time, and she knew it wouldn't be the last. Once again, another woman was laying claim to her husband because he had given her reason to think he was available, that he needed her, and was unhappy in his marriage. Lizzie knew he was not unhappy, but what she didn't know was why he was doing this. Why did he want so many other women in his life when he acted so in love with her? He was doing this because Larry was a serial lover, having many affairs over the course of their marriage.

The Fling

Moving along the continuum, we come to the next affair in which the man feels some sexual attraction to the woman. His affair is mainly a diversion, and one that many men feel they can end whenever they want. He feels he can control it and keep his wife from ever finding out. A man can have one or even a few such affairs over the course of his marriage. Flings are somewhat time-limited—most just fizzle out.

CHARACTERISTICS OF A FLING
- Typically easier to resolve related issues.
- Usually only a few flings over the course of the marriage or relationship.
- He has a very minimal emotional connection to the affair partner.
- Typically easier to resolve than other types of affairs.

The Long-Term Threat of the "Other Woman"

There is little to no emotional connectedness on the part of the man in the fling. However, sometimes the man may begin to feel more emotional connection to the woman, and the affair may become a *romantic* love affair. A serial lover is looking for an affair, while the man having a fling is not looking, but becomes aware when someone starts flirting with him.

When confronted with the discovery of a fling, many men say, "It didn't mean anything." But it *does* means something: To his wife, it means betrayal. What her husband is trying to convey, however, is that there was no emotional connection in the affair. That is what the fling has in common with the serial affair—no emotional connection. The fling can end and the issues that led him to cheat can be easily resolved, whereas this is harder to do with the serial affair.

Where Do Flings Happen?

Flings can happen wherever a pair can meet and feel an attraction for each other. The meeting place is the crucial point—the one at which they can start to flirt and show their interest in one other, or just go their separate ways. Fifty years ago, when suburbia was being developed and most women were stay-at-home moms, the Saturday night cocktail party or neighborhood get-together provided the setting for the beginning of affairs.

A FICTIONAL FLING

The memorable and frightening film *Fatal Attraction* was about a fling that Michael Douglas's character had with Glenn Close's character. He was not looking, but she came on to him and he responded.

Research that was done more recently by the late and well-known psychologist Shirley Glass shows that more extramarital affairs are happening at work than ever before. The workplace is the perfect incubator for affairs: People work closely together and see each other in favorable circumstances (they are dressed nicely, showing off intellectual prowess, and unhindered by their spouses or family members). When interests peak, there is no need to arrange clandestine meetings. You just come to work the next day and he is there. Of course, flings are not necessarily limited to the workplace.

Claudia and John

Claudia was outside the front door when she heard the phone ringing inside. Trying to balance the large grocery bags that were slipping from her hands, she frantically searched for her house keys. Packages were falling before she finally opened the door. The insistent ringing of the phone worried her: *Something might be wrong with one of the children!* It seemed an ominous sign.

She was right in part, but it was not a call about the children. It was her husband's secretary, calling once again to deliver the message that John "will be working late." This had been going on for weeks—this, and the way he rushed to answer his cell phone at odd times and walked away from her to speak to the caller. Her father had been unfaithful to her mother, and Claudia knew the signs. She confronted John, but he denied it. Still, she was certain. They had been married fifteen years and he was always home for dinner at six on the dot. That is, until a few months ago. The private calls on his cell phone at first were infrequent, but their number had increased. She knew it was an affair.

Stunned, she dropped the rest of the groceries and sat down heavily on the sofa. Why? Why is this happening?

Claudia was right, John *was* having an affair. The affair was a fling.

The Romantic Love Affair

This is an affair within which the spouse and the other woman have a very strong emotional connection to each other, as well as sexual attraction. If they both experience the affair as a *romantic love affair*, they will be thinking of each other almost constantly. He will notice himself fading out of his marriage more and more as he becomes more deeply intoxicated with his new love interest. *This affair is so serious that it becomes more important to him than his marriage.* It is so strong that he struggles with the decision of whether to stay in his marriage or leave. The couple in the affair feels a decision must be made because they cannot go on like this: They must marry or stop seeing each other.

CHARACTERISTICS OF THE ROMANTIC LOVE AFFAIR

- He is very emotionally connected to the affair partner.
- It is painful for him to make the "stay or go" decision.
- He experiences guilt if he leaves his marriage.
- He experiences depression if he stays in his marriage.

The Long-Term Threat of the "Other Woman"

If the couple having the affair feels they cannot make either choice, they may continue seeing each other and move up the continuum until they find they are in a *long-term affair*. In this kind of affair, the man is in love with the woman he is having an affair with. *The romantic love affair poses the greatest threat to the marriage.* A man may start the affair for any one of many reasons, but ends it because it is too painful for him to continue if they can't marry.

A POSSIBLE REAL-LIFE LOVE AFFAIR

Prince Charles and Camilla Parker-Bowles may have had a romantic love affair. Charles probably felt Camilla to be his true love and that he had to leave Princess Diana regardless of the pressure he felt as heir to the throne.

If he makes the decision to stop the affair and stay in his marriage, he may become depressed over the loss of the woman he loves. This kind of man is not as controlling as the other men who have affairs.

Bridget and George

Bridget was crying as she sat in her therapist's office. Her husband, George, had ended his affair of ten months.

BRIDGET: *I thought I would be so happy that the affair was over. I felt we would be happy again, but we aren't. He is depressed. I sure know the signs well enough. I've been depressed myself over this. He mopes around the house when he is at home. He hardly talks to me. He tries to act differently around the children, but it is that forced laugh. What is going on?*

The therapist gently explains to Bridget that Perry is depressed over the end of his romantic love affair and that it will take a while for his depression to lift. However, they both can be helped to understand why he had the affair. Perry also can be helped to grieve for the loss he feels from its end, and Bridget to understand that the decision was to stay with her, and to help her rebuild her shattered self-esteem. Together they will work to rebuild their marriage and make it strong, maybe more so than it was before. What she should remember is that Perry made a choice to stay with her, and together they can work through this.

DEGREES OF ATTACHMENT

This section shows that affairs vary in the degree of connectedness to the other woman. In some cases, the feeling of attachment is very strong (romantic love or long-term affairs). In other cases, it is weak (the fling or the serial affair). In the case of the serial affair, the man has no attachment to one person, but is unable to stop having affairs.

The Long-Term Affair

The *long-term* affair is rare, but it does exist. This term describes couples who continue their affair with the understanding that they will not divorce their current spouse(s) and marry each other. Their affair becomes a *parallel marriage*. His first and second family may know of the existence of the other. Many of these affairs can develop and thrive because the partner lives out of town, so the man does not have the problem of the two women meeting.

CHARACTERISTICS OF A LONG-TERM AFFAIR
- The affair becomes a parallel relationship.
- His wife may or may not know.
- His wife may find out only after his death.
- His children are hurt and also feel cheated.
- His children, as adults, may continue to search for answers.

The Long-Term Threat of the "Other Woman"

If family members know of the affair, then the other woman has a significant impact on their life. If family members don't know, they have many questions about why the parents act differently than others they observe. As one woman told me, "My sister and I felt our family was strange and finally when we were older, we figured it out. We have a lot of personality and social problems because of our childhood. There were too many secrets and too many questions that were not answered honestly. My sister and I are very angry at our father and also our mother. Growing up in a divorced family would have been better than this deceit." The lives of all members and extended members of the family are impacted very negatively from a *parallel marriage*.

SECRET LIVES

Sometimes, men can keep long-term affairs a secret until they die. At that point, the secret is sometimes revealed in his will, where he may have provided for the second family (and some, a third) in some way. This was the case with the couple in Anita Shreve's novel *The Pilot's Wife*, in which an airline pilot had a second family in London, with children.

Lila and Patrick

After dinner, Lila and Patrick sit down in their living room to watch the news. Lila puts down her needlework and speaks to her husband.

LILA: *I don't want you to make any plans with Becky for Sunday evening, the twentieth of March.*
PATRICK: *Okay. Why? Something up?*
LILA: *Yes. I am planning a dinner party here so that we can meet the Fishers before Amy's wedding. I'm inviting a lot of family members on both sides. Jack's sister is planning a wedding shower and we will give an engagement party. There will be lots of festivities. I don't want your Becky to call here and I don't want you to make calls to her from our house during this period. I want you to be available.*

Amy is very nervous about the whole thing. The Fishers don't know anything about the arrangement we have. So I don't want Becky to call here that day or night or any other time until the wedding. Okay?

PATRICK: *Of course. I know the agreement.*

LILA: *Father Clary is going to have a special Mass Sunday morning for Amy and Jack. I want that to go well. It should be a happy time.*

PATRICK: *Of course. I am sorry that this is how things have turned out, Lila.*

Their daughter's wedding should be a happy time for Lila, but it isn't completely, because her husband isn't "there" as she had always wished him to be. He is preoccupied with his "other wife," Becky, of eight years. This was the solution to the affair because Lila and Patrick couldn't agree on divorce as a solution. Patrick is a man with two families. He is having a *long-term affair.*

WHY IT'S IMPORTANT TO UNDERSTAND CONNECTEDNESS

This knowledge of affairs provides a framework so that you may be able to see where your partner's affair is on a continuum of connectedness to the affair person. Then you may be able to understand the emotional connection of your husband or partner to his lover and you can begin to see the affair occurring not in isolation, but in relation to other issues.

Stages of an Affair

Just as it's crucial to know what type of affair your husband is having, it's also important to understand the stages of an affair to better understand your husband's behavior. I know it may be hard to read this, but knowledge is power. Knowing the stages may help you get an idea of where he is in his affair.

Affairs proceed in these four stages. They may overlap, but essentially, they proceed in this fashion.

Stage 1: Attraction

This occurs when the couple notices one another, starts to flirt, tease, and be playful with an underlying promise of the sexuality to come. They each may try to find out the marital status of the other. For some, it does not matter—they are already flirting. They show a keen interest in one another that soon segues into the next stage, which I call the *honeymoon.*

Stage 2: Honeymoon

Sex starts at this stage. The couple has a full-blown, active affair with secret meetings, exchanges of gifts, and clandestine trips. They keep in touch by cell phone and e-mail. This is the stage of intoxication, almost an addiction-like process, in which they are preoccupied with thoughts of each other and are very sensually aroused by being with each other. The secrecy of their meetings heightens this passion and increases their obsessive thinking about one another. They think of themselves as a couple and start to celebrate anniversaries, give gifts, send messages, and buy things together. This can go on for months or years. She becomes his "lady-in-waiting." She is on-call—"just a phone call away."

Stage 3: Disequilibrium

This stage is characterized by arguments and discussions about his leaving his marriage to marry her. There are ultimatums, promises made and broken, and general discontent. The deadline dates come and go. It may be that he is ambivalent about her, or is uncomfortable with intimacy or their being together. He may know that he is never going to leave his family, but withholds this information from her. Instead, he gives her yet more deadlines, such as a child's approaching graduation or marriage or "after Christmas." Dates are set for him to leave his wife, but the deadlines come and are unheeded. She gives ultimatums and they are not honored. Most important, he may perceive the affair as a fling; she, as a romantic love affair. Things are falling apart. They enter into the last and final stage of the affair. They are searching for an answer.

Stage 4: The Answer

The couple must come to a decision. The negatives of the affair are beginning to outweigh the positives. They have three choices: to marry, to break up, or to continue and have their relationship become a long-term affair. Another possibility is that he unconsciously becomes careless and leaves clues that his wife discovers, and then the affair ends. This is the point where an answer is reached. Usually, however, the affair just fizzles out. Remember, the chances of his marrying her are very small.

The Impact of the Affair on Those Involved

Now, let's look at the effect of the affair on all three people involved. In general terms, the affair raises the man's self-esteem considerably and lowers the wife's. The other woman is always waiting for him, for his calls, and for his decision to leave his family. Even if the affair is short-lived, it takes years to erase the effects.

His Point of View

The affair is very different from love at home. He anticipates it with high expectation. The fact that it is secret adds to the excitement. There are no interruptions from children, no budget discussions, no problems to discuss. More than likely, there is candlelight, flowers, a drink before dinner or a quiet dinner out, and then their sexual tryst. It could even be a walk together and then a stop for something to eat. He is living in a bubble. It becomes a haven for him, and he feels very good. He feels powerful and in control. Most important, his self-esteem rises. While the man is usually not interested in marriage to her, he also is not interested in leaving the affair until she starts putting pressure on him to marry.

The Affairee's Point of View

She plans her life around him and his activities. She curtails many of her own activities because she must be ready if he can get away or suddenly has time to see her. She has a cell phone by which she can be reached. She must change plans if he has an emergency and he needs to be with his family. If she has an emergency, however, he is not usually available to help her. She sacrifices her future for him, but usually doesn't realize it.

Her main defenses are rationalization and denial. She believes that he is miserable in his marriage; it's permissible to have an affair when he is so unhappy, it doesn't hurt anything, and in the end he will choose her, because she makes him so happy. She denies that he stays in his marriage because he wants to. She views the wife as the source of his unhappiness and as her rival. There is very little sympathy on the part of the other woman for the wife. Yet according to Annette Lawson in her book *Adultery*, fewer than 10 percent of individuals involved in an extramarital affair will leave the marriage to marry that person.

Your Point of View

Discovery that one's husband is having or has had an affair is shocking news for most women, resulting in strong emotional reactions. Your first reaction is disbelief, followed by anger, rage, and depression. You are likely haunted by the betrayal, and you constantly review this event in your mind. With understanding support and the skills you need to help you through the very bad time, you will come to accept that it happened. You and your partner may choose to begin to restructure your life together after you understand why this happened so it is not likely to occur again. Though it is painful, this crisis can result in a stronger marriage.

How to Confront Him about the Affair

I generally feel that if you suspect your husband is having an affair and want to approach him, it's a good idea to do so. Following are details about situations in which it's not a good idea, as well as how to approach him properly.

When Not to Reveal Your Suspicions

I do not recommend confronting your partner about a possible affair if he has a history of physical violence (hitting you, pushing you, or throwing things at you), is verbally abusive (screaming at you, calling you names, or making threats), or is emotionally abusive (won't speak to you, ignores you when you speak, belittles you, or disappears for days without telling you where he is going). It's also not a good idea to confront a man who is addicted to drugs or alcohol, or who seems to have serious problems even if you don't know what they are. If this is the case, seek professional counseling by yourself and work on the issue with the help of a therapist.

When and How to Reveal Your Suspicions

If you suspect your husband or partner of having an affair and he does not fit into the previous category, here are the steps to take in your talk with him:

1. Prepare by going over in your mind what you want to say. Be as relaxed as you can.
2. Pick a time when there will be no demands on your time or his, no possible interruptions, and time to talk. Do not answer phones if at all possible.
3. If he comes home in a bad mood, wait for another day.
4. Find a comfortable place to talk.
5. Try to calmly state your suspicions.

If your partner denies the suspicions, you can say, "I am angry, but I am trying to stay calm and I will tell you why I believe this." In Chapter 11, you will read more about effective communication.

Quiz

1. Since a fling does not have a lot of emotional connectedness, it is not a significant event in the marriage. Yes/No
2. Seeing prostitutes isn't a threat to the marriage because it is a "guy thing"—there is no emotional connectedness, and there is no danger he will run off with a prostitute. Yes/No
3. A romantic love affair is a serious threat to a marriage. Yes/No
4. The long-term affair causes great danger for the relationship. Yes/No
5. Affairs do not hit as hard when one partner finds out about it after the death of the partner. Yes/No
6. Affairs have a better chance of ending at certain stages than at others. Yes/No
7. It is easier to end an affair in the last two stages, because of the disillusionment with the affair. Yes/No
8. If you suspect an affair, speak to your husband about it. Yes/No

Answers

1. **Yes.** Even though there is little emotional connectedness, a fling must be taken seriously because it is a betrayal. At the very least, it presents an opportunity to discuss infidelity and how you feel about it. It is also an opportunity to see if any problems are brewing in your relationship.
2. **No.** He is a serial lover, and that is a threat to your marriage. He may not run off with a prostitute, but that's simply because he does not want to be with any affairee permanently. Seeing prostitutes cannot be excused as a "guy thing." A serial lover cannot make an emotional connection to anyone. He may be a sexual addict, and could be at high risk of exposing you to a sexually transmitted disease.
3. **Yes.** It is, because he has fallen in love with another woman, and is considering leaving your relationship. This is very difficult for both of you and for the children. Very serious discussions should occur.

4. **Yes.** It does, even when the man doesn't divorce or end the relationship. (Often, this is because the woman will not agree to a divorce for religious or financial reasons.) They can become bitter strangers. Often, the children from each family are curious about each other and want to meet.

5. **No.** The surviving partner who does not know is deeply hurt when discovering an affair after the partner has died, and it is sometimes hard to recover from such a discovery at that point. She had not had an opportunity to speak with him, to question him, to express personal feelings. The partner is left to sort it out, to question events, and to work out an answer. She can still, however, gain some understanding of why he had the affair.

6. **Yes.** During the first two stages, the man is so flattered, intoxicated by the attention, and has such a rise in self-esteem, he is less interested in leaving. What helps it end is his guilt, his feeling about affairs, his attachment to his children, and what is going on in his life. These feelings are more apparent in the final two stages.

7. **Yes . . . or No.** The answer is usually "yes," but occasionally a man is unhappy in his relationship and sees no way of fixing it. Therefore, he may end the affair and the relationship even if the affair has progressed to the last two phases.

8. **Yes.** It is always beneficial to speak about your suspicions or knowledge of the affair. Be proactive in participating in discussions with him about the affair, but realize, it is more difficult in Stage 2 than at other times. Effective communication is very significant.

   However, *if your partner is a volatile man who becomes violent, do not confront him*. In that case, work with therapists who specialize in domestic violence. The affair is not as important as your safety. *Do not question him on your own.*

chapter two

NONPHYSICAL AFFAIRS

Now that you know that affairs differ in intensity based on their attachment or degree of connectedness to the affair person, you need to know that there is another way to categorize different kinds of affairs. These are variations on the traditional affair "theme"; that is, there are ways to have affairs that are a result of technological and social changes. It's important to identify them and understand their meaning, because they are tricky, in that they may not seem to be what they are.

Nontraditional Affairs

The affairs we discussed in the previous chapter are usually referred to as "traditional affairs," because such affairs have been going on throughout human history and because the lovers physically touch each other and have sex. In recent times, two newer kinds of affairs have been recognized. These are referred to as "nontraditional affairs" because they differ considerably from the traditional affair. One is called the *emotional affair*, and the other is called the *cyber affair*.

The Emotional Affair

An emotional affair is one in which there is no sexual behavior toward one another, but the two parties desire it. Instead of physical passion, there is a chemical attraction and there is intimacy. The couple does not usually talk about this, and so there is no commitment.

Emotional affairs are dangerous and I consider them to be a serious threat to the marriage even if they do not become sexual affairs. His preoccupation with another woman is taking substance from you and your family. If the emotional affair becomes a sexual affair, we would describe it as a traditional affair and on the continuum. It would most likely be a romantic love affair. They already have the glue of a love affair intimacy and having added sex to their relationship, they now have passion.

Indications of an Emotional Affair

The signs of an emotional affair are much harder to determine than those of a traditional affair. The signs are subtle even when you are looking for them. If you suspect your partner is having an emotional affair, ask yourself these questions:

- Does he seem more preoccupied or remote than ever before?
- Does he work overtime and weekends much more than he ever did?
- Has he stopped talking to you about work?
- Has his personality changed, without it being due to any circumstances of which you are aware?
- When he does talk about work, does he mention one person's name more than any other?
- Are you having less time together and seem not to enjoy each other's company as you did before?

If you have answered "yes" to more than half of these questions, there may be a problem he's hiding from you. It does not necessarily mean he's having an emotional affair. It may be that there is a problem at work, or he is concerned over something else that he has not shared with you.

What Does an Emotional Affair Offer Him?

As we search for the answer to why he cheats, we know that if it is an emotional affair, he desires the *intimacy*. He is enjoying being adored by another, feeling special, and having excitement in his life. This person has time for him—time to listen empathically, time to hear all his concerns, and time to react to him respectfully.

This is also someone who doesn't see him at home in a different role with other responsibilities. She doesn't see him take out the garbage or perform other household responsibilities. She sees him on the job, doing his best and earning the respect of those around him. Working together on a common goal creates camaraderie. She may have sat next to him as they worked together on a project while having takeout when no one else was there. Such a setting is different from that at home, and can be conducive to closeness.

The Origins of Emotional Affairs

As women flooded into the workplace in the 1960s, '70s, and '80s, they started meeting men they would never have met at an earlier time in history. Now, almost every place where there is work to be found, women are there too. They work closely with men as equals and sometimes as their superiors. They interact in ways not even imagined by their mothers and grandmothers.

They may stay at work late into the evening, going over their projects together with men. Work becomes very close, personal, and intimate. They may become emotionally close as they work on the same goal, and soon the physical attraction for the other is realized. It may not be long before one or the other *could* act on their feelings.

Many wives are not certain their husbands are having an affair when it is an emotional affair because they believe the woman is a colleague, but they do wonder why he has to work late so often and sometimes has weekend meetings. When a husband is having an emotional affair, the wife is fading away from him because he thinks obsessively of the other person; he saves stories to tell her, fantasizes about being alone with her, and is always afraid of talking too much about her or even uttering her name. The emotional affair is "one slip-up away" from a sexual affair. Physically, they will "accidentally" touch each other or put an arm around the other, but they do not have sex, even though that is what they want.

Bonnie and Ron

Bonnie and Ron came into my office because Bonnie thinks Ron is having an affair with his research assistant.

BONNIE: *Ron has been working very closely on a high-priority lab research project with his research assistant, Jan. I know the work hours are unusual because of the urgency of the project, but I still don't like it. But last week he and Jan went to Atlanta for a conference about this project. I could never get him on the phone while he was away. He called me, but I couldn't reach him when I called. Something is wrong and I am beginning to think he is having an affair with Jan. I confronted him and he swears that isn't true. He even said I could see her at the lab's Christmas party next week.*

So I went and I could see from their interactions that they were having an affair. When we got home we discussed it and he told me he was very attracted to her, but it was not an affair. I was so upset and that is why we are here.

I then asked Ron to come in the next week with Bonnie and when he did, I asked if he could tell me about his relationship with Jan.

RON: *We have a close relationship. It is related to work most of the time. We do talk about some personal things, but we don't have sex or even kiss. We haven't been intimate. It's not **that** kind of relationship. I am hurt that Bonnie would even think that.*

Do you have thoughts of holding Jan or kissing her?

RON: *Yes. But that is nothing. I don't do it.*

So, you fantasize about her.

RON: *Yes, yes, but I have never made a move on her.*

After more discussion, Ron realized how very involved he had become with Jan; and finally he said:

RON: *I told you we haven't been intimate. **I haven't had sex with her**, but I do want to. I am so sorry, Bonnie. I am very ashamed.*

This was very hard and very embarrassing for him to acknowledge. Ron acknowledged he was having an emotional affair, and one that could be on the verge of becoming a sexual one. Ron was trying to assure his wife that they were not having sex, which he often referred to as "intimacy." His relationship had all the hallmarks of an affair, except for not having sex. They have *emotional intimacy*, which means that Ron and Jan are comfortable with each other and with sharing their most private thoughts and stories. Emotional intimacy is a very pleasant feeling of closeness, trust, and safety with another person. Emotional intimacy is a very important component of love. People think of intimacy as being a sexual relationship. With emotional intimacy, you feel you can share all your fears, weaknesses, and thoughts without being personally criticized or rejected. You are accepted for who you are.

Once he did make that connection, Ron was able to begin work on understanding how that happened and to work with Bonnie on their relationship. He was also able to end the emotional affair with Jan, and to set up boundaries for himself in their working relationship.

What to Do If You Suspect an Emotional Affair

To find out if your partner is having an emotional affair, ask him during a quiet time when there are no interruptions, and when you show concern and a willingness to listen. Use the same guidelines that were described at the end of Chapter 1. If the answer is "yes," that he is having an emotional affair, remember it is not yet sexual, but it is serious. You can nip it in the bud, but you must find a therapist to help with this and to help restore the closeness in your relationship.

The Cyber Affair

The second variation on the topic of nontraditional affairs is the cyber affair (also called *cyber infidelity* or *cyber cheating*). This is an affair that occurs by means of the Internet. Online sexual behavior is called *cyber sex*. Technology has provided a new and simple way for people to meet via the Internet, and quick ways to keep in contact with each other through cell phones and by texting. All of this communication occurs electronically, without touching each other. Just as with an emotional affair, a person in a committed relationship or in a marriage breaks their vows by having an affair online.

The Mystique of the Internet

Many people cannot understand how a couple can have an affair online when they can't see or touch each other. It is a mystery to many, but when you understand some of the special properties of the Internet and the psychological responses to them, you can better see how such a relationship can develop. Let's look at three of the properties of the Internet so that you can get a better understanding of its power and mystique.

Triple-A Engine

In 2000, psychologist Alvin Cooper described the Internet as having three properties: Accessibility, Anonymity, and Affordability. He notes that nothing else offers these three properties in one device, and together they add up to a phenomenon never seen before. The technology of the Internet allows people to find their own personal ways of using its properties.

- **Accessibility:** The computer can be used by anybody at any time and in any place. Planning a rendezvous on the computer is easy. Even if the other person lives in Russia, Israel, or Argentina, meeting up online is as easy as it would be to meet a friend three miles away. Friendships that develop at work conferences or meetings don't have to end even if the person lives three states away. When a couple is using the computer for an affair, they can meet more easily, without much planning. No appointments need be made. There is no need for special clothing, salon visits, or planning where to go, and it is not as time-consuming as meeting in the real world. No one sees you. You can be talking and doing your nails. Your hair can be wet and you can be in your PJs.
- **Anonymity:** People can hide or change their real identity when meeting others online and then continue their cyber relationship. They go online using a pseudonym or a screen name, which can be seductive and send a message in and of itself. They can try out different personalities, pretend to be someone else other than who they are, and they can lie about the facts of their lives. A person can

assume the personality and personal facts of someone he admires or would like to be, and present this persona to anyone he meets online. Despite all this potential for falsehood, people still become attracted to others online. The person they "fall for" may be a combination of their projections and the untruths that are told.

- **Affordability:** Online dating or affairs are very inexpensive: There is only the cost of the Internet service provider. There is no cover charge, dinner expenses, theater tickets, hotel costs, special clothes, or any of those extras associated with an evening out. Anyone from anywhere can go anyplace at no cost with little chance of being caught. If it doesn't go well, ending the evening is only a click away.

The Attractions of the Internet

The following are attractions of the Internet that cause people to enjoy an affair even with a person they don't know. Because it is a real person responding, it is different from watching pornography. You can see how the following characteristics could easily fulfill someone's needs.

Pseudo-intimacy

People IMing (instant messaging) each other on the Internet feel as though they are the only two people on earth. This makes them feel very close to one another. People feel safe online in these private encounters. To them, this feels like emotional intimacy. That is the major attraction of the Internet for people having a cyber affair. But it is not true intimacy, because that can only be experienced in person. This intimacy felt online is called *pseudo-intimacy*.

Projection

There can be a significant misinterpretation of the message online, due to the process called *projection*. Online, there is a deficit of the auditory and visual clues that we are accustomed to in person-to-person interactions. This deficit is compensated for by one's imagination and through projection, by which the traits wanted in a lover are projected onto the words one is reading. Projection occurs when one person imagines the other to have certain physical or personality characteristics desired in a partner, rather than what he or she actually may be.

For example, if a man had a stern and critical mother who impacted him negatively, online he will be looking for the opposite. He may put a different slant on the text he reads from his cyber lover. Everything is left to the imagination. It could also be, for example, that a woman wants a strong man and so she creates one by her interpretation of the words her online partner types. The combination of the pseudo-intimacy online and the magic of projection produce quite a strong aphrodisiac.

Safety

The Internet imparts a feeling of safety to cyber lovers because no one else knows what they are doing. No one can see them or hear them. They feel they are alone and protected. Of course, they may not be safe at all because they do not know anything about each other besides what they type on their computers. They may not be, or do, or feel what they communicate in their e-mails or IMs (instant messages). The Internet creates a feeling of safety even though it can be a very dangerous place.

What comes through during the communication may *seem* the essence of that person, but that may not be true at all. One could be talking with sexual predators, con men, or even someone they know who has kept his or her true identity a secret. Some users of the Internet lie about their gender, age, religion, race, and the facts of their lives. In a traditional affair, much of this can be seen.

In addition, cyber lovers probably lack a frame of reference. When a person you know in your hometown tells you he likes a certain club or restaurant, you know something about his taste because you are aware of those places. When someone in the virtual world tells you about a club, you know nothing about its reputation, the kind of people who attend, what the club's purpose is, or, for that matter, whether it even exists. In the real world, when you can see the person, the degree to which he lies or distorts who he is becomes more obvious than it does online. Worst of all, you do not know what he does with what you type. He can send it to anyone around the world. This alone has caused pain and misery to many.

Lies

The Internet hides everyone's flaws. Lovers meet in unusual circumstances, and they can't see each other. Many overweight individuals report they are ignored when they go out and feel that people are not interested in what they have to say. Online, however, others are interested in them and they don't feel left out as they do at parties and groups in the real world.

This happens, as well, with the shy person who is willing to speak out on the computer, where safety from embarrassment is only a click away. There are people who find personal chatting and small talk difficult when face to face but have excellent writing skills that allow them to turn on the charm online.

UNDERSTANDING NON-SUBSTANCE ADDICTIONS

When a person is having an affair online, it is important to know whether this is a case of infidelity or sexual addiction. Many don't understand how a person can be addicted to something that is not a substance that can be seen or ingested like alcohol, cocaine, or food, but is produced by the body. Please see Chapter 9 for more information about sexual addiction. Although it can feel frightening to believe that a spouse is sexually addicted, it is important to know the difference between cyber infidelity and sexual addiction online because the treatment for each differs.

Cases of Cyber Infidelity

In a cyber affair, it is most likely that the individual has been using the Internet for communicating with one person and their relationship has become very important. He most likely met this person in a chatroom online. If they then meet offline, their affair becomes a traditional affair and the Internet is used for communication and sex.

Let's look at the differences for comparison, as we continue our quest to understand why men cheat.

Glen and Jill and Their Cyber Affair

Glen met Jill in a chatroom for married men who are looking for fun. They have been having cyber sex for three months. Glen lives in Manhattan Beach in California, where his partner, Karen, is a scriptwriter for a comedy show and he is a stay-at-home dad who writes technical scientific manuals. Jill lives in Alexandria, Virginia, where she is a speech pathologist and her husband works at the Air and Space Museum.

It's gray, dreary, and cold outside, not the typical Southern California weather, but the kind that seemed to permeate the inside of the house as well. Glen quietly leaves his bed, being careful not to wake Karen, who is softly snoring beside him. It is hard for him to awaken at 5:00 A.M. but he must in order to IM Jill at 8 A.M. on the East Coast. He goes to the den, turns on the computer, and is in contact with Jill, whose husband and children have already left the house.

GLEN: *hey*
JILL: *hey urself*
GLEN: *r u looking great today*
JILL: *glad u can't c me, bad hair day*
GLEN: *dreamed of u last night*
JILL: *problem today, bobby jr has practice for big game tomorrow & is home*
GLEN: *bummer*
JILL: *thinking of u a lot*
GLEN: *of what*
JILL: *your great body, where do u want me 2 touch u*
GLEN: *start with my strong arms & work down*
JILL: *running my hands down ur strong back along yur muscles to. Bobby jr just got up gg [gotta go]*
GLEN: *:(ICLY [I cyber love you]*

They both click off their computers. Glen and Jill were interrupted because of her son's early awakening. When not rushed, they exchange some news and information about events in their lives. Then they

IM in ways to sexually arouse each other and themselves as well, by describing their bodies, the way that they feel, and use language that will cause the other to be aroused. While doing this, they each touch their own bodies for arousal and they masturbate. This process is a way of having cyber sex with each other.

How did this happen? They are two people who have never met. What can explain their attraction? The connections that people make with each other on the Net happen extremely fast and can be very strong. Earlier, we discussed the properties of the Internet; now we must look at the human side of this arrangement to understand the power it exerts on people. The attractions of the Internet make it very easy for some people to become sexually addicted to Internet usage who would not have been sexually addicted without it.

Mary and Gregg

MARY: *I don't know where to start and I don't know what to do.*
THERAPIST: *Start anywhere. You can fill in anything you've forgotten or left out and soon will have a picture of what your concern is.*
MARY: *It's more than a concern.*
THERAPIST: *I know. Go on.*

Mary rummages through her large bag and brings out an envelope filled with almost a hundred e-mails that Gregg sent to women and their answers to him.

MARY: *He is corresponding with a lot of women and they speak . . . ugh . . . ugh . . . very dirty to each other.*

THERAPIST: *What are you feeling about this?*
MARY: *Anger, rage. I showed it to him and he said they were noth-ing. Just fooling around. I am worried. He used to go to massage parlors before we met. What should I do?*

The therapist asked Gregg to join Mary so that they could begin to understand what was happening. Later that day, the therapist saw another woman with a somewhat similar story.

Lisa and Neal

LISA: *I was home one night doing my computer class homework while Neal was playing cards with his friends. My assignment was to learn how to organize and transfer files. I found a file that at first confused me until I realized that I was reading e-mails that showed Neal was corresponding with a woman in Connecticut. We've been married seven months and he was having sex online.*
THERAPIST: *That must have been very upsetting. Have you spoken to him about this?*
LISA: *He said I spend too much time at school and with my studies. He said he picked a site for friendship and then just started "going private" with this one woman. Soon they left the group and were more in touch with each other only. He said they haven't had cyber sex, they really only communicate as friends.*

Although these two women are seeking a therapist for a problem they are experiencing with their husbands' online activities, the men are probably using the Internet to help them cope with two different issues. Gregg appears to be sexually addicted and uses the Internet for that purpose, while Neal is using the Internet for something similar to an emotional affair. They are both dangerous affairs that can jeop-ardize a marriage, and must be attended to by a competent mental health professional.

Now that we have explored the types of traditional affairs, the variations of affairs, and the stages of affairs, let's review it by taking a quiz, and by doing so learn a little more about affairs.

Quiz

1. Seventy-six percent of men have affairs. True/False
2. Couples who discuss their views of infidelity before marriage are less likely to have affairs when they marry. True/False
3. It is important to know the type of affair your partner has. True/False
4. The affairee is usually more attractive than the wife. True/False
5. Sex is better with the affairee. True/False
6. Cyber sex is not really sex because they don't touch and they don't know each other. True/False
7. You shouldn't start therapy unless he apologizes. True/False
8. The workplace is conducive to having affairs. True/False

Answers

1. **False.** Research by Dr. Shirley Glass in 2000 shows that 25 percent of women have had an EMA (extramarital affair), while 44 percent of men have had one. This is consistent with results of other research such as the Janus Report (1993), which shows 26 percent of women and 35 percent of men having an EMA. Interestingly, the numbers have remained rather consistent since the 1953 *Kinsey Report*, with 26 percent of women and 50 percent of men reporting an affair then.

2. **True.** Annette Lawson's research reports that there are fewer EMAs when men and women discuss their feelings concerning infidelity before marriage.

3. **True.** Some affairs have a better prognosis than others. Knowing the differences can help in your decision-making on how to deal with this event in your life.

4. **False.** Reports show that the wife is convinced of that. However, many wives are surprised to discover that the lover is usually not better-looking than she is.

5. **False.** Reports show that the sex is often better with the wife than the affair partner.

6. **False.** Cyber sex is sex. Individuals are very sexually stimulated during their encounter and they typically end by masturbating. Like

the more traditional affair, the husband keeps it a secret and does not say to his wife, "Okay, honey, I am going upstairs to mutually masturbate with this woman in Utah."

7. **False.** Infidelity is a difficult issue to work on by yourself. It is important to receive help for it. The apology will eventually come. If it doesn't, the therapist will want to understand why, and work on that issue until you are satisfied one way or another. Remorse on the part of the husband is significant.

8. **True.** In a study of workplace affairs, 55 percent of husbands and 50 percent of women had **not** had previous affairs.

chapter three

WHAT IS LOVE MADE OF?

One thing is certain: Love is complicated! So many components go into creating and maintaining love. In this chapter, we'll identify and analyze those components so you can determine whether a breakdown in any of them may have contributed to his affair.

What Is True Love?

In 1988, psychologist Robert J. Sternberg, in his book *The Triangle of Love: Intimacy, Passion, Commitment*, created a model of love that is very helpful in understanding relationships, both committed and affairs. He used a triangular concept with passion, intimacy, and commitment each being one leg of the triangle of true love. Without any one of them, there is no triangle, and no true love. The components develop between men and women in a specific order, just as they are presented here: *passion* first, then *intimacy*, and finally *commitment*. In early stages of an affair, only passion is present, but as the couple spends more time together, there is a chance for intimacy to develop. Let's take a look at each in greater detail.

Passion

A couple's married or committed life together starts with the vows they make to one another. At this point, most couples are enthralled and in the first stages of love, when they are intoxicated with each other. Sternberg has called this first stage *passion*. They think of each other almost constantly; they are obsessed with each other. Sternberg uses the phrase "crazy in love" to capture the level of passion. It is the excitement and the intoxication with each other that characterize this component. Although all components must all be present at the same time for true love, they start at different times in their relationship.

Passion rises quickly and is sustained for a while. However, passion doesn't last long at such heights because couples cannot sustain it over the course of time in any relationship. So, it drops to lower levels. Therefore, passion later in the marriage is not as intense as the passion in the early years.

Some people do not see this decline of passion as normal. They feel that when passion cools, they have fallen out of love with their partner or their partner has fallen out of love with them. They come to the conclusion that the honeymoon is over, and this conclusion causes a lot of concern and worry. Some people are more susceptible to having an affair at this time because they have lost that "intoxication" that drew them to their partner.

Refusing to acknowledge a drop in passion, however, is not an emotionally mature way of looking at what has happened. No couple can sustain such high levels of passion for a very long time. That is why therapists encourage couples to normalize these feelings and to work with them on rejuvenating their marriage. It's important to remember that having to work on a marriage does not mean the marriage is a bad one.

The decline in the heights that passion first reached means the couple must bring more sexual excitement to the marriage. They may be in a rut, but that doesn't necessarily mean they are out of love with each other. People who are bored and don't understand what happens in marriages may think that love is gone. For some males, this is intolerable and they have an affair to make themselves feel better.

The following statements may show the decline in passion that naturally happens over the course of a relationship because the initial fascination is gone and because people work very hard and are tired:

- She doesn't seem to want to have sex as much.
- She is always too tired for lovemaking.
- Something is wrong. He doesn't react to me when I am all dressed up to go out.

When a person has an affair, that feeling of intoxication that he has missed is now present again. He is thrilled to have recaptured passion, but he needs to understand that he probably has not fallen out of love, and should not panic. The marriage is settling in and the decline in passion means the marriage needs a tune-up. It doesn't mean he has to look outside the marriage for passion.

Intimacy

The second stage in Sternberg's concept is *intimacy*. This is really the glue of a relationship. Intimacy is the emotional component of his model. Intimacy describes a feeling of safety and trust with each other, and people need time to develop that level of trust in another person. Intimacy can reach heights as high as passion, but takes a little longer to do so. It is present in a relationship when one can be oneself and still be loved and respected. The couple can share their weaknesses with one another and can still be accepted, cared for, and loved.

Intimacy is very important as it relates to affairs. According to Annette Lawson, a British sociologist, married women have affairs primarily because of a strong need for intimacy. Intimacy is a very important need for women in any of their relationships. If she has an affair and finds intimacy, she could leave her marriage because this need is so great. In fact, lack of intimacy is a greater threat than any other to her marriage.

Intimacy poses a different problem for men. Men are raised differently: As boys it can be difficult for them to achieve intimacy with other boys and later with women. As grown men, they can have difficulty making the commitment of marriage because of this issue with intimacy. They understand it differently than women do. Many men and some women as well believe intimacy to mean having sex, not the emotional closeness I have described.

These statements show there may be a problem with intimacy:

- We eat dinner and watch TV at the same time, but we have nothing to say each other.
- Bob ignores me when I tell him about something I am upset about.
- Jim is cold. He'd rather talk to his friends about a game than with me about something I bring up.

When the woman *wants* intimacy and the man cannot trust enough to be intimate, he may feel so threatened that he has an affair. An affair walls off the wife and creates the distance between husband and wife that reduces his anxiety over their closeness.

To be intimate, there must be trust. After the revelation of an affair, women hold back their love because of a lack of trust. They are vigilant in checking the mail, and looking at phone records and credit card bills. It is hard to re-establish intimacy after an affair because trust has been broken, and it takes a long time to repair. It can be, but must be worked on.

Commitment

The third stage is *commitment*. Just like intimacy, it reaches high levels, but takes longer to do so. Commitment is a promise to always be with each other. It can continue throughout the marriage.

Stresses such as aging, illness, or disabilities may weaken the bonds of commitment in a marriage. Not everyone can face up to the vow of "for better or for worse." At this point, the man's commitment may waver, especially if either passion or intimacy is also reduced or missing. With the advent of erectile dysfunction medications, more men than ever before are able to be sexually active as they age—making a man more of a "commodity" for older single women. His sense of "being wanted" can add to a weakening in the commitment to the marriage.

The following statements show issues that are warning signs about commitment and about the marriage itself:

- Bob likes to take vacations alone all the time.
- Jake visits his family and never takes me.
- Mark takes all the money and gives me an allowance.

Passion, intimacy, and commitment all are important, and the absence of any one tells you something about the state of true love in your relationship. It's important to understand these three components if you want to know more about the causes of his affair.

Internal and External Worlds

We have looked at a picture of couples and love, types of affairs, and the stages of an affair. However, couples do not live in a vacuum. They are affected by the world in which they grew up and the attitudes, goals, and values they saw during childhood. Did they accept or reject them? What did they think as they left home and were exposed to other thoughts? These two people bring to the marriage a family history as well as a personal one.

The Internal World

In order to get a complete picture of your relationship, try to determine what was valued by each of you before you married. It's vital to understand the expectations you both brought to the marriage and whether or not they were realistic. You can learn what was significant in your families; how your values were shaped by your parents, siblings, and the events that occurred in your family, *even before you were born.*

If these expectations were not met, was the marriage affected in any way? For example, if one of the partners expects a family-centered life and the other a more social life, the possibility of stress exists. This stress can be one of the factors that may result in his having an affair.

Additionally, since very few couples live in isolation, we need to know how well the integration of each set of parents and the couple has gone, as well as the impact the parents and other family members may have had on the couple. For example, has the merging of families created tension with your mother-in-law, problems with a domineering father-in-law, sibling rivalry, or general antagonism in the family? All of this can create a hostile environment for the couple. Will these situations influence the expectations of the marriage?

To decide, we need an understanding of the couple from a generational view. For instance, if he comes from a family in which his grandfathers, father, and uncles had affairs, this history may increase the risk for him (or other members of his family) to have affairs. On the other hand, some men may disapprove of the previous generation's infidelities and will not repeat that behavior. See Chapter 5 for more information on men with a family legacy of affairs.

From our family, we learn rules and roles and we go out into the world with these. You will see as you read further how this is played out in life and how it can cause problems. For example, a young man who was idolized and the center of his parents' attention may learn to believe that others should treat him that way; that was the family rule. There also may be other rules, such as "men come first."

Roles are also given to family members, including loser, winner, dope, scapegoat, or martyr. As children grow up, they play out these roles (often unconsciously) and they can consistently (and again, often unconsciously) put themselves in these roles in their relationships. Many of these roles and rules cause them problems outside the family if they do not challenge them. They also can play a part in affairs, and so we must be aware of them.

Another major part of this picture is the occurrence of one or more stressful events a few years before the affair. *Family events, major transitions, illnesses, dreams that failed, and disappointments can set the stage for an affair.* Much can be learned by exploring these factors, as well as the general state of the marriage.

The External World

The external world is everything around the couple, from their neighborhood to national problems, the times in which they live, and the social problems they see. How do they integrate the internal and external and come out with their own view of the world and how they want to live in it? Before we explore the reasons that cause affairs, we must complete this picture of how each person was formed by an internal and external world and how the resulting view meshed with that of his or her partner. Then we can relate it to affairs.

The world around us is instrumental in our formation, just as was the experience of growing up in our families. For example, a family is greatly stressed when one of the couple is absent from home for protracted periods of time. These separations, such as those caused by incapacitating illnesses, incarceration, and geographical separation, are very stressful. Both parents and children are anxious when this happens to anyone in the family.

Understanding the meaning of the affair must take many things into account. There is not a simple answer because it differs for each couple. It is a puzzle and you must put all the pieces together, such as each person's background, values, desires, transitions, the families, and what your life together is and has been like.

Other needs and pressures can keep a couple emotionally apart, such as the use of drugs and alcohol, or intense interest in a hobby—like the man who spends all his free time on his woodworking project. Then there is the fan who goes to every sports event in his city, the man overly involved in work, and the one who can always be found on the golf course. Likewise, a woman can become overly involved in her work, school, hobbies, or other interests that keep her physically or emotionally engaged somewhere else. Some of these behaviors may be due to a lack of intimacy.

The economic recession beginning in 2008 provides an example of how an outside event can put pressures on a family. Every day, the reports of more layoffs in what once were strong companies sent fear through many households. Large bank closings were frightening enough to hear about, but the sheer numbers of smaller bank closures made everyone's life seem unstable. Worried as well were those who had grandparents who had lived through the Great Depression, and heard tales of families who could not feed their children. The message was clear: The economy was in trouble. As a result, many people were on edge. Family life was affected by it. Even children were aware. The loss of a job for a person who considers himself or herself a "breadwinner" is a traumatic event.

External events can have enormous effects on individuals. They often bring *change*—and change in itself can cause anxiety.

Stages That Affect Our Lives

As we grow, there are two stages of changes that all of us go through. As individuals, we go through **adult** developmental stages of life, but as a family, we go through changes known as **family** developmental stages. Both of these stages can have an impact on love and the marriage, even though some factors may have occurred long before the individuals met. Knowing about both individual and family developmental stages is more information needed to help you understand the affair. This information is another piece that fits together with others, and gives a more complete picture of what motivates each partner. Then we will have the background to better answer the question of "Why did he cheat on me?"

Adult Life Stages

People don't usually spend time talking about their adult life stages; they just get on with it and live their lives. But when you are trying to learn about infidelity, you need to know what most people expect from life and where the greatest blows can occur, because stress can lead to an affair. Dr. Erik Erikson wrote in 1950 that starting at birth, we will go through developmental stages until the end of our lives, and he writes that we have goals to accomplish throughout life. In his concept of the adult stages of life, in **young adulthood**, we leave home and find those things that are important to us—our work and our partner in life. In the next stage, we put our efforts into our **career** and **raising our family**. In the last stage, we **retire** and give back to the community, and review our life for a sense of integrity before the end of our days. For many, it is a struggle to find one's true love, and for others a struggle for the right career, even though we now recognize that people may have two or three different careers in a lifetime.

Your parents have experienced some of these stages and continue to do so as they go down life's path. Their stages overlap with your stage, making a complex structure of the family *through the generations.*

It is important to be aware of this because stress can appear with your parents, children, and you and your mate as these passages are negotiated. Enough stress and discontent can be the preconditions for an affair. Stress goes back and forth through the generations. Keep this in mind as we look at the stages of family life.

Family Developmental Stages

Families go through stages as well. Just as individuals go through the developmental life stages, the marriage also goes through stages. People and families in their early years differ from the later ones. These changes can affect the three legs of the triangle of true love. Let's look at how the couple goes through changes.

- **Establishing Their Life Together:** In their first stage, the couple tries to get to know each other and establish a home for themselves. They may or may not have children. The partners spend their first years building intimacy. They form friendships that might add to the ones they individually had before their union. They begin to establish boundaries between their life and that of their parents. These can be trying goals for new relationships.

- **Building a Family:** This phase will take years to accomplish. The couple's world is very busy with their work and the needs of children.

- **Launching Children:** The period of raising children, which can be difficult, is followed by launching the children into the world. For some this is a joy; for others, not. There are many points in this phase that can cause anxiety for the pair. Each couple responds to this time of life differently. Some miss their children and the always-present energy they created in the home.

- **Renegotiating Their Lives Together:** This is a tricky period. Many men will soon see that their relationship with their partner has changed as well. The couple will need to adapt to having more time together. This is a big adjustment. Some feel they have more free time to do what they enjoy, or find new activities they can share. Others, however, find that they have grown apart or changed and they are uncomfortable being together. They have been so involved in running the family that now they are like a CEO without a job. At this point some want to separate and see what their life would be like. Others experiment with an affair. It is a time when many couples are troubled and enter therapy for help for the emptiness they feel. This period also occurs at midlife and when families are coping with the needs of older parents.

- **Retirement:** This is also a very tricky period, depending a lot on what has happened in the previous phase. People today are typically happier during retirement than were people in previous generations, but the danger of an affair is not over, for the same reasons that are present during the previous phase.

How These Stages Impact Fidelity

At any given time, a couple is dealing with several layers of developmental phases at once:

- Each partner is in a certain developmental life stage.
- Each set of parents is in a particular adult and family developmental stage.
- The couple is in a certain stage in marriage/family development.

All of these phases interact and intersect, and any one or more may be responsible for stress in the relationship. Once you've identified where the stresses may be coming from, you can speak about them with your partner. When the two of you have a mutual understanding of the issues at hand, you can determine how you will manage the stresses created by your internal and external worlds.

MEN AND WOMEN AND THEIR DIFFERENCES

More men report having affairs than do women. Psychologist Shirley Glass conducted research that shows that 25 percent of women have had affairs, as compared to 50 percent of men. These statistics have been consistent since 1953, when Dr. Alfred Kinsey made headlines by publishing his famous *Kinsey Report*, which detailed his research on the relatively new field of human sexuality and startled the world with the results of his study: 26 percent of women, as compared to 50 percent of men, had affairs. This era followed the stress of the Great Depression and World War II when everyone's minds were on family, building suburban homes like Levittown in New York, and leading a peaceful existence. They wanted to live the new American dream, and high statistics of infidelity did not fit in with the ideal world they were trying to create after such turmoil. Why, for at least the last sixty years, have 50 percent of men had affairs as opposed to 26 percent of women? The answer has to do with the difference in how each gender views intimacy.

Women and Intimacy

Most women who have affairs are searching for intimacy—something they are used to and have craved ever since they were children. How do little girls learn about intimacy? Carol Gilligan, a well-known Harvard psychologist for nineteen years and now on the staff of New York University, is noted for her work on the social differences between girls and boys. In her book titled *In a Different Voice*, she writes that when a little girl gets into an argument with a girlfriend, she packs up her dolls and goes home to talk to her mother about it. She might tell her mother that her playmate has hurt her feelings. Her mother sympathizes, and then the girl begins to feel better. She grows up and has girlfriends and they talk with each other, tell one another secrets, and share their special thoughts. Teenagers see their friends in school and talk with them whenever they are able—on the bus, in homeroom, at lunch, walking to class, and then on the bus going home. When they arrive home, they talk to each other on the phone for hours. (Or, today, they are likely to *text* each other for hours.)

Either way, women communicate. Talking makes them feel better, and they continue this when they grow up and marry or have careers. They meet their friends for lunch or for dinner, and they talk. Women know the art of intimacy and will tell you that they love to get together with their woman friends. Even though they may be busy moms or career women, they still want to see each other. They feel intimacy from sharing their problems, they empathize with each other, they support one another, and they let each other know that they are there for one another.

Men and Intimacy

Gilligan writes that when little boys run into problems while playing, they don't go home and talk to their moms about it. They huddle and solve the problem; feelings don't get into it. Nobody talks about his hurt feelings, and no one stops speaking to the others. If one boy feels misunderstood, he is quiet about it, and goes on with the game. They learn from this to problem-solve without empathy. A lot of camaraderie is exhibited by laughter, hitting one another on the shoulder, or "high-fiving." Most of the time, when they are upset, they don't discuss their emotions. They either get angry and yell, or throw their caps down or, in the common vernacular, they just "suck it up."

When they grow up, they still want to be with their friends. They go to a sports event, have dinner, or go out for a drink. They greet each other enthusiastically and their talk is very light—maybe politics, sports, work—but with most men, it is not about personal problems.

How a Difference in Intimacy Can Lead to an Affair

Because they had such different experiences with intimacy as children, men and women continue to approach intimacy differently as adults, too. As problems happen, the modus operandi for men is to problem-solve by themselves. For women it is to talk about it and to be understood.

Most men don't want to discuss problems—they want to do something to solve it. When they hear the TV isn't working, they're right on it to fix it! If a man's wife has a scheduling conflict, there he is in the car, driving the kids around.

His strategy, however, is not always a healthy one. A problem that's bothering him emotionally may benefit from discussion, even if it is a problem that can't be solved. If he feels the excitement is missing from the marriage, he doesn't discuss it. Instead, he switches TV channels. When she says that he isn't romantic anymore, he nods. When she tells him he doesn't surprise her with gifts, he gulps and continues reading the sports section. She is giving him a clue about her dissatisfaction, but he doesn't recognize it as such.

Intimacy is the emotional component of love.

The root emotional problem, when added to other issues such as those at work, or with older parents or young children, can grow. The combination of these situations can feel overwhelming and could possibly be a factor in infidelity. When partners do not discuss the issues, the problems in the home grow in intensity and the family atmosphere becomes heavy with resentments. Partners argue, make snide remarks, and use sarcasm: The tone in the home becomes tense, and the bad feelings continue to grow. Even if some of the resentments are past history, they use constant reminders, such as that she insisted on buying the house or he picked the lousy neighborhood, which continue to wear down both husband and wife. Both are unhappy, as anyone would be, living in this type of atmosphere.

When the atmosphere of the relationship deteriorates in this way, the man may become so disconnected from his wife that he turns to another woman to get away from the stress.

What Intimacy Means to a Man's Affair

Because of these differences in how men and women approach intimacy, they also experience sex differently. Men can have sex without an emotional connection to their partner. That is why, when talking about the affair, men can truthfully say that it "meant nothing." It is impossible for women to make sense of that statement. I have seen men who deeply love their wife and who are dismayed by her response to their infidelity. They can't understand why she doesn't believe that the affair really did mean nothing.

When a man says, "It means nothing to me" or "I don't know why I did it," that may well be true. These, however, are not excuses; they are red flags that say you must find the reasons for the affair or the cheating may happen again.

He may also say he doesn't know why he did it, and this statement can be true as well. When he says he loves his wife, that too is true. He knows that he likes the release and response he has to sex, but doesn't connect it to anything else in his life.

In contrast, women need to have a strong emotional connection or be in love to have sex.

Differences in Sex Drives

It's no secret that men and women have different sex drives. Years ago, Ann Landers asked her readers, "Would you be content to be held close and forget the 'act'?" Of the 90,000 women who answered her question, a whopping 70 percent answered "yes."

Clearly, sex means different things to men and women. For men, it means feeling manly, powerful, and in control—not feelings that a woman craves. At the end of lovemaking, he has a release from tension and feels wonderful. He feels like he "broke the bank at Monte Carlo." Women, however, have different expectations from sex. First, a woman wants to have sex with someone she loves or cares deeply about. Having sex makes her feel loved, desired, special, and protected: None of these feelings are on a man's top ten list. At the end, she has a release from tension and feels good and peaceful. Women who speak of the satisfaction they receive from their sexual life talk of husbands who show their love in many ways, including being affectionate, loving, and playful when they are alone, as well as being loved. When they are in bed, these women know they are loved. Women enjoy sex, because they love the hugs, caresses, and tenderness they receive from their husbands as well as the lovemaking.

Some women who come to my office have described how wonderful an orgasm makes them feel. The unfortunate part is that about 40 percent of women do not have orgasms. It is easier for a man to feel manly, powerful, and in control from an affair, because orgasm is what happens to him during sex. On the other hand, women, who need tenderness and intimacy from their partners, will not have an affair as easily as a man. They simply aren't likely to look, and even if they do, they are less likely to find someone who can meet those needs. Often, a woman who has sex with a man who cares little or nothing about her reports that those needs are not met, and that she feels as though she were being "used."

A Man's "Cure-All": The Affair

We have seen that most women try to solve their problems by talking them through. They go to support groups, talk to their friends, read books on the topic, or go to a therapist. We also know that men do not like to do those things. Then how do they deal with their tension? Yes, some get together with the guys or exercise. But most men look toward their almost universal release: sex.

Is there anyone alive who hasn't heard that infamous phrase men use—"What she needs is a good lay"? A man is likely to see sex as a solution for whatever the reason he has an affair. He may be dealing with a problem of his own, or one that you have, or one in the relationship. If he is unable to solve the issue, he resorts to what makes him feel better—and that is sex. He picks another woman because it brings excitement. No matter how short the affair may be, it offers some temporary help. The woman may mean nothing to him and he may not know why he is doing this. He has probably thought nothing of the consequences, but the "good lay" has come to be a cure-all in men's view.

AN ESCAPE

For him, the affair is an escape and a way to cope with problems he doesn't know how to solve.

When the tensions from these issues build up, this cure-all becomes an option for men to consider. In the beginning, he finds the attraction of the affair exciting. He thinks about her all the time, and he anticipates sex with her. He is back in the *intoxication* phase of love, but the other two phases of love are missing. He is feeling passion without intimacy or commitment: *in other words, not love.*

He feels he is in a honeymoon period. His self-esteem increases with her, just as it does with any new romance. He is living in a bubble, because there are no responsibilities, problems, or arguments. In the affair he doesn't come home to problems. Their clandestine romantic meetings are all he has to be concerned with—just being in the moment. The secret nature makes it even more exciting, and he thinks he has found a way to cope with the stress. The irony is that his cure-all is *not* a cure at all, but a temporary release that brings more anguish to everyone.

Exercise

It's time to do an assessment on your partner's affair based on what you've learned in Part I. The answers are only for you to look at. Remember, there is no right or wrong answer. The purpose is recognition and understanding.

Contributing Causes to the Affair

1. Are any of the components of true love missing from your relationship? Yes/No
   If so, which one:
   Passion? Yes/No
   Intimacy? Yes/No
   Commitment? Yes/No
2. Remembering back, can you tell when any of these components started to slip away?
3. Can you see a reason? Yes/No
   If so, what was it?

How Might Your Husband Answer?

Now try to guess how your husband would answer the same questions. Put yourself in his shoes and be as objective as you can.

1. Are any of the components of true love missing from your relationship? Yes/No
   If so, which one:
   Passion? Yes/No
   Intimacy? Yes/No
   Commitment? Yes/No
2. Remembering back, can you tell when any of these components started to slip away?
3. Can you see a reason? Yes/No
   If so, what was it?

Stresses

Stress impacts our sense of well-being, and if it accumulates, it could result in an affair. Think about stress in your life as a couple as you answer these questions:

1. Were there any stressful issues that occurred in your family or marriage in the **two years** preceding the affair? (If so, list them.)
2. Would you say that things on the list could cause stress? Yes/No
3. On a scale of 1 to 10, where would you place the sum total of stress (when 1 is a stress-free life and 10 is completely stress-filled)?
4. Do you think this stress contributed to your husband having an affair? Yes/No
5. What factors in **your** childhood or background influenced your view of marriage?
6. In your opinion, what factors in your **partner's** childhood or background explain his view of infidelity?
7. What family rules may have caused **you** difficulties in life?
8. What family rules may have caused your **partner** difficulties in life?
9. Are their any family **roles** that may have caused **you** difficulties in life? Yes/No
10. What family **roles** may have caused your **partner** difficulties in life?
11. Have there been any stresses that you and your partner have experienced since you took your vows that you consider an explanation for the affair?
12. In reading this chapter, what did you realize about your and your partner's internal world?
13. In reading this chapter, what did you realize about your partner's external world?

Understanding why your partner cheats requires a review of your internal and external worlds, and the way they helped you form and internalize your values and behavior. This is valuable information as we go on to learn more about affairs.

Part II

WHAT CAUSES AFFAIRS?

"While I am sure that many of these relationships are deep emotional bonds, it is worthy of note that you hardly ever see beautiful young women with poor or unimportant men."

POWER: THE ULTIMATE APHRODISIAC, BY DR. RUTH WESTHEIMER AND STEVEN KAPLAN

"Seduce her, however, and at one stroke you removed not only her clothing but her honor and, of course, her remarkableness, thus rendering her just another woman in another bed."

MISTRESS OF THE ART OF DEATH, BY ARIANA FRANKLIN

chapter four

TRANSITIONS

We are now going to look at the causes of affairs that most families cope with. Our first stop is to look at transitions and their effect on our lives. Life is a series of transitions, and affairs can sometimes occur as a result of the stress they cause. Some affairs based on transitions have a good chance for a positive outcome; others do not. We'll start with those that have the best chance for a good outcome, and proceed chapter by chapter to those with less chance.

In the previous chapter, we talked about individual and family stages in life and how any stress from them could make people more vulnerable. Under certain conditions, change can cause stress. You have no doubt heard of a groom who had a fling on his wedding day, or the man who had an affair on his honeymoon or when his first child was born. Such transitions happen merely as a result of living, but for some men, the stress of such a change causes him to seek an affair. We will try to understand this by looking at his internal and external world and what the transition means to him in light of this information.

What Is a Transition?

Dr. Nancy Schlossberg tells us that transitions are events in our life that can be *expected, unexpected, off-time,* or those that produce *ongoing stress*. All of these cause a change in the way we look at ourselves and our place in our world. Let's look at the transitions.

"On-Time"/Expected Transitions

All the steps in the family developmental stages discussed in Chapter 3 are expected transitions: They are changes in life. They can bring a little anxiety with them, even though usually we look forward to them—the wedding, the new baby, or retirement—because we will be taking on a new role. However, even when taking on a new role that we want, there is still some stress because of concerns we might have. We know the old role but not the new one, even though we want the new role. For example, a man may be very happy about getting a promotion, but worried that he can't perform at the higher level; he knows the old job, but is a little insecure about the new one.

A Non-Event

A non-event is also a transition, something we hope will happen, but doesn't—like never getting married, or being childless. Unlike expected events, these non-events can cause a considerable amount of stress, unhappiness, and depression. Individuals may react strongly to that stress, and some may have an affair.

NON-EVENTS ARE STRESSFUL, TOO

Things that do *not* happen can change our lives as much as those that *do* happen. By definition, a non-event can also be a transition, because it is a change in the way we think about ourselves. The definition says it changes our world as well, and is a loss of our dreams. This is something a person usually finds very painful, but must adjust to.

Unexpected Transitions

An unexpected transition is one that you do not think will happen to you—for example, a divorce or the breakup of a committed relationship. Others might include your husband being arrested on drug charges, a dissolution of a business partnership, or a fire that destroys your home. Imagine a man who worked hard for years to earn enough money to build a business, which had been a dream his father had for him. The man had grown up in poverty and envisioned the business as a way out—only to lose his money in the recession beginning in 2008. His stress came from the failure of his internal messages to materialize the wishes of his father. No one who knew this man would ever expect him to have an affair, but the blows of the non-event (the business he was unable to build) were hard for him to manage. This does not condone his affair, but we must know this information to understand him and help him and his wife recover.

Consider the situation in which a couple cannot conceive a child. The stress may differ in intensity for the couple who have no options versus the couple who can adopt or benefit from the advances in fertility treatments. A couple may, of course, try to adopt, but that is not an option for everyone, and it still is not the way they wanted parenthood to happen. If the couple cannot become parents by any means, they must begin to think of themselves differently. The couple had the stress of dealing not only with the possibility of no children, or difficult and expensive fertility treatments, and maybe the unexpected situation of the husband wanting a divorce; they now must put aside their dreams and face the new reality. There is no new baby to take home; no first birthday; no first steps.

In a group I was leading, a sweet and very attractive woman, whom I will call Ginger, shocked the group with her story. She told of working in the early years of her marriage to put her husband through medical school until he graduated, specialized, and established his medical practice, and then they could afford to have children. When they reached that goal, she discovered that after years of not conceiving, and spending over $40,000 on infertility treatments, he was having an affair and was going to leave her to marry a younger woman "with a younger uterus." This stressful transition caused by a non-event (their inability to have children) apparently caused him to have an affair.

This couple did not reconcile because Ginger's husband did not want to. She told me more stories that showed how self-centered he was. In her therapy, Ginger had to grieve for the loss of her marriage and her dream of children with him, and had to restore her self-esteem. She went back to work for the law firm where she had previously worked, fell in love with a lawyer, and married him. A few years later she dropped a note with a picture of the little boy they adopted.

Off-time Transitions

There are also *off-time* transitions. On-time transitions are those that are expected at a certain time in life, such as in the life and family developmental cycles; off-time transitions happen either **before or after** the expected time.

For example, children often leave home at about eighteen years of age (on-time), but if they leave at thirty years, it is considered off-time. A couple who is still trying to launch a child of thirty into the world is experiencing an off-time transition, just as their child is. Their plans are changed or put on hold. They think of their lives differently than do people whose children left home at the expected time. The adult child becomes the center of their attention; they avoid friends because their lives are so different, and holidays become depressing for them. If, on the other hand, a child leaves home at age fifteen, that is also off-time. Home life stops as they put all their efforts into finding that child, and dealing with their fears of abduction, bodily harm to their child, or running off with her teenage boyfriend. Both of these situations produce considerable family stress.

Ongoing Stresses

Other situations also can be considered transitions, even if they are ongoing. Chronic health problems, long-term unemployment, and serious financial issues are examples of such stresses. Although the situations are ongoing, with no short-term end in sight, they cause the people involved to think about themselves and their world in a new way. Thus they also are called transitions.

For example, a family member with a debilitating illness or an elderly parent who needs constant care creates a transition for the family because they now have **a new view of life**. They have undergone a transition, and with it the stress and anxiety that accompany difficult medical situations. Because medical situations can change frequently, the people involved may experience multiple transitions as a result of the initial one (perhaps an elderly parent moves in with the family, then later needs to move to an assisted-living facility, causing stress or guilty feelings).

Or, consider a man who has been unemployed for a long period of time. His situation may also cause stressful situations for other members of his family (perhaps his wife has to begin working again, or take on more hours), thus prolonging the effects of the initial transition (his unemployment). These types of ongoing transitions add more stress to a situation of ongoing stress.

It is important for us to understand ongoing transitions, since there are cases of infidelity that are caused by the stress of a transition. The degree of stress depends, in part, on how the individual perceives the transition. If the transition is ongoing, the stress may become chronic. Not only do transitions cause anxiety; they can also result in depression.

Support Systems and Transitions

A transition is a family situation. It affects everyone, and family life is not the same during and perhaps even after the transition. The caregiver is under a strain most people can't imagine. For example, Harry, a man whom I had counseled five years ago, returned. He started telling me about his wife, Helen, who had seen him through a difficulty, and then he started to cry. Helen had developed multiple sclerosis and their lives had changed and would only get worse. He started listing the problems and sobbing almost uncontrollably—they had school-age children, Helen couldn't drive, cook their meals, and was losing more of her abilities. I interrupted and asked him what he wasn't telling me. He answered, "I'm having an affair." This man had never had an affair before, but this ongoing condition at home led him there. He found a very poor remedy for his despair.

What Harry needed was support. I helped him cope with his depression and learn how he and Helen could still be a couple under these circumstances, and also helped him learn how to talk to his children. I referred Harry to a social worker, who found aides and organizations to help him. Harry no longer felt so alone; he no longer needed the affair and gave it up readily. We both agreed that he should not tell Helen of the affair because of her medical condition.

See Chapter 11 for more information about communication skills.

THERE IS HOPE

Transitions can cause anxiety, and some people find a solution to this anxiety, as we have seen in these examples, by having an affair. Remember that in Chapter 1 we defined an affair as a *maladaptive solution*. Most affairs caused by transitions are *flings*: They mean nothing to the husband. They were a way to control the anxiety he was feeling, but at its basis, it is an emotional issue that he cannot cope with. That is why these affairs are typically easier to cope with than some other types.

Coping with these transitions, whether planned or unplanned, positive or negative, require a person to assess his life by looking at his assets. As he faces a change, he will look at what assets he has in terms of support, whether from family, friends, therapists, support groups, religion, or institutional programs designed to be helpful. He must also check his attitudes and the belief systems that have developed, and see if they help or hinder. Our thinking can lead us into despair. For example, this is a conversation Harry and I had about Helen's multiple sclerosis:

HARRY: *Helen and I can never have fun anymore.*
ME: *What did you like to do?*
HARRY: *We liked to go to dinner, the movies, dance, play bridge, travel. I don't know . . . stuff like that.*
ME: *It seems to me there is a lot you can do. You won't be able to dance, but you can do all the other things, even travel. There may be adjustments you make, like getting to the movies early to be able to settle into a seat comfortably. I am going to give you a list of places and organizations that will help you, and place you in a support group.*

Harry was beginning to feel the way he thought. Everything was negative. Harry jumped to conclusions and made assumptions. He filtered out the positive entirely. This type of thinking is called cognitive distortion, but he and everyone else can be taught to recognize this and to confront the distortions. Research shows that cognitive therapy combats depression and that individuals can learn how to do this. This is a very valuable tool. Check out Chapter 11 for more information.

If Your Partner Had an Affair Because of Transition

If your partner's affair is the result of a transition, you may be able to work through this situation. There can be a good outcome from affairs due to transitions, because the couple can learn effective communication skills, empathy, cognitive skills, and strategies to reduce stress now and in the future. As you read through this book, you will find yourself learning skills and strategies that will help you. Many of them will be taught in detail in Part III. These skills can help the man manage stress instead of looking outside the marriage for a stress release.

Now let's continue our discussion of the more important transitions, and how to deal with them, by looking at some case histories. We will review two cases of affairs during transitions so that you can see not only the complexity, but most important how to cope with them.

Esther and Brian

It was a gloomy morning when Esther and Brian, a thirty-something couple, entered my office. Esther was darting looks of anger at Brian. She would not sit near him. She sat with her arms folded across her chest and started to tell me her story. Her demeanor soon changed from anger to tears.

> **ESTHER**: *I just found out about this the day before yesterday. I am so furious and I am hurt more than I can say. Brian's been having an affair with a twenty-one-year-old girl. We have eighteen-year-old daughters! I find it disgusting!*
> **BRIAN**: *It was wrong, but I hate to think of it as disgusting or me as disgusting.*

Esther and Brian were married the summer after they graduated from high school. Esther found out she was pregnant in May, a month before graduation. They didn't want to share the news with anyone, so they married in a small family gathering at her home, followed by a dinner at a local restaurant.

ESTHER: *It wasn't the wedding I dreamed of, but I was so in love with Brian then—and I still am—that I thought I could handle it. [She started crying again.] But we found out we were going to have twins. It was almost too much to absorb. It was embarrassing, but at the same time we were thrilled. They were born two months early, which made it difficult for us, knowing the "month counters" would notice. But still, we were happy. Our lives became so different than our friends'.*

BRIAN: *Yeah, our friends went off to college and we were really kids ourselves, raising two little babies. It had its own rewards, even though money was always tight.*

Brian's View

After our first session together, I had a private session with each. I learned from Brian that when he graduated from high school, he felt desperate. He had won a scholarship to a prestigious art school, but even with that money, they couldn't manage unless one of them worked, which wasn't possible given that Esther was pregnant with twins. He did love her and still does.

This couple initially was coping with an *off-time transition*—an unplanned pregnancy that interrupted their plans for themselves at another transition point in life.

BRIAN: *We had another child three years later, a little boy. Those first nine years were busy with child care and trying to support the children. Don't get me wrong—they were fun, but there has always been a struggle.*

I asked what he would have done if he had gone to college. Brian's posture and facial expression changed and I knew this would be significant information.

BRIAN: *I would have studied art. I love to paint. I tried to continue, but oils are so expensive and time was so short, I couldn't. I've been working at an art store framing pictures. It's very upscale and customers always ask for my opinion on the frames, but it is not as satisfying as painting. I don't know where my life has gone. If only Esther and I had waited and I finished college, things may have been different. We would have had kids later and we both could have worked.*

You can see that Brian had another major life transition: a non-event. He was not going to be the artist he had dreamed of being. Brian was at an individual developmental point, the midlife point where he would be evaluating where he is in life versus where he wanted to be. He felt like a failure and saw no future for himself.

I asked him about the affair.

BRIAN: *There is no excuse. I knew what I was doing. I just wanted to feel good, to be with someone who really liked me, didn't tell me about problems day and night. Esther is worried about how we will be able to send two kids to college at the same time for three years and then we will have three at once for another year. She never stops talking about it. I guess because I don't know what we will do, it is killing me. I feel such a failure. Jenna works in the store and is interested in art and is fun to be with. I really feel good and forget everything when I am with her. I have ended it with Jenna and I won't do it again, but I have caused a lot of damage.*

Esther's View
The next week, I spoke with Esther alone.

ESTHER: *I know Brian and I missed out on a lot of fun by marrying so early. We were raising a family when others were in college. Now I am going to school to be a paralegal and I expect to be working in three months. That will help. I know I am not going to leave him. I love him and to leave would have a horrible effect on the children. And on him, too. He is nuts about the kids. I think this has been about our family life. We don't speak nicely to each other anymore.*

Overview of Their Issues

Brian's affair was a fling with a coworker, and it has ended. Brian is still depressed and anxious, however, due to his two significant transitions; one at high school age when he had intended to go to college, and a second at midlife when he believed his career dream would never materialize. Even though the first transition happened eighteen years ago, it still affects him and has seemed to put a stranglehold on him. It is important to deal with the causes of the affair *regardless of whether they are current or in the past.* He can deal with it by expressing his disappointment over what had happened. Brian and Esther had to have that long-overdue conversation in which he poured his heart out to her and she listened and understood him, and let him know that. Esther had to have the same kind of conversation. They had to listen to one another and make the other one know he or she was understood. Apologies had to be exchanged, and they would answer each other with understanding. This is a powerful beginning.

Brian feels like a failure both in his career and as a husband and father. To him his future looks bleak; he sees no way to change the course of his life. He and Esther have little fun. While having his affair, Brian felt happy, desired, and seemed less anxious. Brian had his affair to dull the pain of the psychological issues he was facing because of not navigating the transitions in life as he had hoped. The affair came just as he was making another major transition: his daughters were leaving for college.

Working Through the Affair

This couple has a chance for a good outcome if they follow these steps. The therapy must cope with the emotional issues: Esther's reaction to Brian's affair and Brian's disappointment of giving up his scholarship and his feeling of loss of a career.

1. First, Esther must cope with her emotions, which is typical after discovery of an affair. She feels betrayed and with that comes rage, shock, depression, anxiety, and disbelief—to name only the most prevalent emotions.
2. Brian, too, has to manage his difficult feelings, such as guilt and depression. He feels hopeless and powerless.
3. The next step is for each to understand how this affair happened. They need to track the events that led to the infidelity—in this case, transitional events or non-events. But they must do things differently than they did before the affair.

Transitional problems like Esther and Brian's can be approached in the following way: Each of the pair talks about their disappointment with the way events turned out. They need to understand the other's view of the issues and to see what influence his or her internal and external world caused. Esther and Brian both came from supportive families, but the parents and the couple felt embarrassed about the pregnancy at that time. The pregnancy was an off-time transition.

A couple can try to deal with transitional problems by making a list of their assets and their deficits. The plan is to make the list and then to brainstorm ways to *increase their assets* and to *decrease their deficits*. To help Esther and Brian, I led them through such an assessment: in other words, what they have got going for them (assets) and what is not working or working against them (deficits). Then I helped them try to increase the assets and decrease the deficits.

MAXIMIZE ASSETS

When dealing with an affair, identify your assets and increase them, perhaps by finding additional social services, family, and friends. Also, be sure to address the impact of the affair on all the family members, because everyone is affected.

Esther and Brian's Assets

- The affair was a fling.
- Brian ended the affair.
- Brian feels remorse.
- They love each other despite the affair.
- Both want to stay in their marriage.
- There is no history of previous affairs, physical abuse, or substance abuse.

Brian and Esther have some very positive assets. The key assets are that they still love each other and that Brian's affair was a fling and that he is very remorseful.

How They Can Cope with the Deficits

- **Poor communication:** Many of Brian and Esther's problems have resulted from inadequate communication. When people use poor communication skills, the situation usually becomes harder to cope with. Brian and Esther will need to use the good communication skills they have begun in counseling to talk about the pain of the affair. They should learn communication skills so that they can share their feelings with each other and express the loss that the off-time transition has caused them. Visit Chapter 11 for more information on communication skills.
- **Emotional pain:** Brian and Esther will continue to deal with the emotional aftermath of infidelity in addition to the stress of their transitions, past and current. During the therapy, they will be guided in how to speak respectfully about what is on their minds, and will learn how to problem-solve when they disagree.
- **Financial strain:** Brian and Esther were given three referrals to select one for their financial counseling. They must also talk with the school counselor about financial aid for the twins in college.
- **Future career uncertainty:** Though Esther is about to get her certification, she is not employed yet. She will ask a career counselor for advice on how to seek work after she receives her certificate.

- **Lack of friendships:** Brian and Esther became isolated when their friends went off to college. To cope with that isolation, they will join church social activities to meet others.
- **Negative thinking:** They will learn cognitive skills as a means of self-help for challenging negative thinking. Cognitive skills are an excellent self-help means of solving problems. It helps identify negative thoughts and teaches a new way of thinking, one that is not confrontational.

This plan helped Brian and Esther learn from the affair, deal with psychological issues that have been plaguing them for nineteen years, and face the challenges of the coming years in a healthy way.

Nonconfrontational Talking

In my plan for Brian and Esther I mentioned identifying negative thoughts. Let's look in on Couple A and B as they discuss where they are going on Saturday night. First, here's Couple A:

ROBERTA: *We are going out with the Millers Saturday night. Where do you want to go?*
JOE: *Nowhere! He is such a know-it-all. Why did you make plans with that idiot? Because you're an idiot. You know I hate him. Call him and tell him that we are not going. And he knows about the affair.*
ROBERTA: *I know he does. Everybody does. You shouldn't have done it.*
JOE: *Cancel it.*
ROBERTA: *Okay.*

There was a lot of name-calling and a general bad tone was set. Let's look at Couple B:

CAROLINE: *Joe, I need to talk with you. I made plans for Saturday night that you won't like.*
JOE: *We're going to a movie and out to eat with the Millers.*

CAROLINE: *How did you know?*

JOE: *Because you've wanted to go with them for some time.*

CAROLINE: *It will be okay. I told Jen we didn't want to talk about it. We have to start sometime. They've been friends for a long time.*

JOE: *Okay. I will try it.*

CAROLINE: *I will make it a short evening and I will be there with you.*

JOE: *Okay.*

This type of compassionate conversation-making is much more productive. Again, see Chapter 11 for more information about communication skills.

Exercise

Here are some questions to ask yourself about your family's transitions. Remember, there are no right or wrong answers. The purpose is recognition and understanding.

1. In the last two years, has your family undergone any transitions? Yes/No
    If "Yes," were they:
    Expected/On-Time: Yes/No
    Off-time: Yes/No
    Unexpected: Yes/No
    Non-event: Yes/No
    Ongoing stress: Yes/No
2. Describe them on a scale of 1 to 10, with 1 being the least stressful and 10 being the most stressful.
    Transition 1: 1 2 3 4 5 6 7 8 9 10
    Transition 2: 1 2 3 4 5 6 7 8 9 10
    Transition 3: 1 2 3 4 5 6 7 8 9 10
    Transition 4: 1 2 3 4 5 6 7 8 9 10
3. In which way would these transitions relate to your partner's affair?
4. List any unresolved transitions from the past that may still be affecting you and your family.
5. For any of your transitions, fill out the following:
    Transition:

    Deficits:

    Assets:

6. How can you decrease your deficits?
7. How can you increase your assets?

chapter five

FAMILY
LEGACIES

It is impossible to understand why an individual cheated without understanding the influence of the families involved—both the family that is coping with his infidelity and the families the couple came from (their family-of-origin). Family plays an important part in our development, in our values, in our married life, and in the way we choose to live our lives. This is true whether you admire the values you were raised with and continue to live in a way that you experienced as a child, or you disapproved of these values and rejected them when you grew up, left home, and married. When you marry, there are two people in the marital bed, but therapists know there are really *four more: a set of parents from both sides.*

The Legacy of an Affair on His Children

When a man cheats on his wife, he cheats on his children as well. Men think that if no one knows, no one can be hurt, or that his children are not affected, but that is false. First, he cheats the entire family of his whole being or presence, of the time he might have spent with them, and the good memories they could have created and treasured all their lives. His children will be as devastated at age fourteen as at age forty when they find out. Second, he cheats his children of a family to model their lives on; instead, they may feel anger and shame. He may cheat his daughters of even more: They may grow up to distrust men and fear marriage, unable to distinguish a man they can trust from one they cannot. Additionally, he may have sent a message to his sons that it is all right to cheat, and in so doing doesn't present a model of what a good husband or father is.

Overt Infidelity in His Family

In some families, the men have affairs, and these infidelities are usually known or suspected by family and friends. The women feel powerless to change what is the family behavior. The behavior of such men is usually modeled on their own fathers and other men in their families, generation after generation. Their sexual liaisons make them feel better about themselves. It makes them feel manlier. They are "one of the guys."They think it is fine to be unfaithful as long as it does not disturb your family. These men are narcissistic, not caring how their infidelities impact their wives and children. Their need to repeatedly prove their manliness to themselves and their pals supersedes everything else. Though the affair is ultimately their decision, they have been raised in a family culture that promotes infidelity.

When children see dysfunctional behavior in their family-of-origin, they have two choices: to continue it in their own lives (that is, to accept it) or to reject it (by discontinuing it). For example, in a family in which two daughters had been sexually abused by a family member as children or young women, one may become sexually repressed and the other one promiscuous. In a family where the father was very controlling, some children may continue that type of behavior as an adult while some may be just the opposite: gentle and considerate. Why would some continue self-defeating behavior and some not? Some make a conscious decision to be different; others do it without thinking or to win father's approval.

Victor, a man from such a family, was devastated because his wife was leaving him due to his many affairs.

VICTOR: *I thought it was the way a man behaved and showed he was a real man. You get together with the guys, high-five each other and brag about your latest. The women didn't know and if they suspected, they didn't care. Everything remained the same. It didn't change things with them. All the men in my family fool around and nobody's wife ever left. But my wife didn't think it was so cool. She was mad as can be and she is planning to leave me.*

Victor made these remarks on a national TV talk show in which I participated, and the women in the audience let Victor know in no uncertain terms how deplorable this behavior was to them. From observing life around him, Victor had grown up thinking this was man's role. It was only the shock of his wife's filing for a divorce that made him think twice about his actions. He said that he loved her, but *"this is how you acted as a man."*

Family Dynamics

In addition to the individual legacy each family member carries as a result of the infidelity, the group dynamic of the family is affected too. When there is infidelity in the family, wives pay a price in how they feel *personally* and how they feel about themselves *publicly*. When a man has many affairs, usually their friends and neighbors know about the affairs and the wife and children live with this embarrassment. If the children do not believe their mother knows, they are torn with concerns about loyalty and what they should do. When both the mother and children know, they may be forced into an uncomfortable coalition with their mother against their father. This plays a role in their development and keeps them from having a happy childhood.

LEGACY OF SEXUAL ADDICTS

Men who cannot stop cheating because they are *sexually addicted* can also leave a legacy to their children. (See Chapter 9 for more on sexual addictions.) Some of the sons of chronically cheating men choose *not* to cheat because they disapprove of it, and they decide on a different, more emotionally mature way to live their lives. Some of the daughters of these chronically cheating men also choose to change the family pattern and are careful to marry men whom they believe will be faithful.

When those children grow up, they must then make their own choices, which is difficult because they haven't been given a role model of an emotionally mature father to emulate. They have to find their way themselves or, if they are lucky, receive help from a mentor they meet along the way. A man who has affairs rarely looks at how he is failing in his role of father. No number of fishing trips with his son will make up for cheating on his son's mother.

How Infidelity Is Passed Down from Father to Son

Men from families in which infidelity is rampant learn these behaviors, which appear to them to be manly, cool, and powerful. Having an affair is, of course, **not** an indication of manliness, but boys and young men may be confused about what makes a real man. Well-known psychiatrist Dr. Frank Pittman writes in *Man Enough* that it is the father's job to help his son understand manhood and how to be a man. He writes, "Men don't sleep around because they have imperfect marriages—they may, but that is no reason to be unfaithful—men sleep around because they don't feel man enough. The roots of infidelity are in the defective relationship between a man and his father—not in a defective marriage."

It is the father's responsibility to be a role model and to guide his son through his childhood and adolescence until he reaches manhood with a sense of ethics. Modeling or teaching infidelity to a son is not "okay." A father should teach a son how to problem-solve, treat others fairly, and have respect for others. A man who seeks affirmation of his manliness by sleeping with a woman other than his wife has not learned how to be a man and, therefore, can't teach his son or be a model for him. Other men in the family or the community can do that for the son, and his mother can teach him proper behavior. Again, when the boy becomes a man, it will ultimately be his own decision whether or not to have an affair himself—but it is undeniable that a son learns behavior from his father.

Covert Encouragement of an Affair

In some families, affairs are encouraged in a more subtle way than in the previous examples. Some messages can be subtle and really are a reflection of someone else's beliefs or needs.

For example, Rita and Perry came to me for couples counseling because he was unhappy in their marriage. Rita was beside herself with anxiety, not understanding what was wrong. She felt she had done her best to have a smoothly running home and to be accommodating to Perry's wishes. During the counseling sessions, Perry was rather nonspecific and vague about his complaints. There seemed to be something missing from this picture.

The missing piece finally was revealed. Perry's father had many affairs and he was now not only encouraging his son to have an affair, but to leave his marriage. Perry's mother told him that his father had wanted to leave her and marry a woman with whom he had been having affair years ago. When Perry reached the same age, his father started encouraging him in very subtle ways to be dissatisfied with his marriage and to leave Rita. His father was acting out his own plans of years ago through his son. When Perry understood this, he was able to assert himself with his father and to put an end to his father's attempted sabotage of his marriage. Then he and Rita worked on strengthening their marriage.

In some cases, to understand family influence, we look at *covert* behavior like that of Perry's father. We find them in their communication, failed plans, coalitions within the family, and the family history. We need to understand the roles of women, the way they are regarded in the family, and whether they are treated with respect or their views and feelings are disregarded.

Family Thinking

In a recent discussion I had with some couples about affairs, this particular group all spoke of how they believed strongly in fidelity and the freedom to enjoy life and relax in the knowledge that comes from having a partner they could trust to be faithful. These couples had been married forty to fifty-three years. Most interesting, given this information about them, is that many of the men at some point in their lives found themselves "tested," when confronted with the possibility of sex with someone other than their wife. They described situations in which they knew someone was "coming on to them" and they could have made it happen if they so desired. All of these men refused the overture. As one explained, the decision would be for the thrill of some excitement, something new for an hour, but not worth the risk they would be taking. Still, they remembered that moment, that decision, forty or fifty years later, as a point in time when something important occurred in their lives.

In individual sessions, women have told me they experienced the same thing. The promise of commitment they made while taking their vows is actually tested some time later in life; for some, this occurs when temptation presents itself. Then one must evaluate what commitment really means, there on the spur of the moment.

One man in the group, Barry, in response to the question, "Why do some men cheat, and others don't?" called out, "*Fear! Fear! Fear!*" Linda (his wife), Barry said, had told him early on that if he ever had an affair, she would leave him.

BARRY: *I didn't think much about what she said until once at a meeting. A very attractive woman was also attending and I knew that if I wanted, I could have pursued it. Then fear came over me. I thought of Linda and I loved her and didn't want to lose her and I didn't want to hurt her. I thought of our three little children, so darling and so precious. I couldn't lose any of this and I couldn't hurt the people I loved. This was not worth the risk. I was afraid of losing what I had, for what? An hour of sex with a stranger?*

Rational Thinking

Barry's answer is an excellent example of rational thinking. Barry did not "wimp out," as someone in the group joked. What he did was think it through in a rational way. This is the way mature people think through their issues, and is the way decisions should be made when they affect others, as it does in a family. "Family thinking" is not linear thinking, as in, if you do A it will affect B. Rather it is like the workings of a clock. Whereas, you do A and it impacts on B and C and D and other parts are then in motion because it is all set off by the first motion. This means that he thought of everyone in his family who is or would be involved in his decision and how it would affect them. He considered the consequences to himself as well. Then he made a decision, after having thought it through. Rational thinking is a mature way of thinking through a situation. Men who have a family history of affairs often lack the ability to think in this rational way.

How Men Rationalize Affairs

Rational thinking, as Barry displayed, is quite different from rationalization. When someone rationalizes, he doesn't face the truth, but hides by excusing his behavior. Rationalization is a way to deceive oneself about behavior that is harmful. Rational thinking is thinking clearly about the consequences of your actions; rationalizing is making excuses for your actions. See Chapter 11 for more on rationalization.

Innocent Fun?

In some families, men get together, go out, and have a little "innocent fun," but the entertainment is not honest and certainly not innocent. It is not the same as women going out to dinner together. The camaraderie is a lie, can lead to a sexually transmitted disease, and damages the marriage even if it is never discovered.

> JANE: *I realized that in our home Jake was a kind, nice guy, but when the family got together, he and his brothers and their cousins drank beer, left the house, didn't come home until late. The next day they would have a card game in the club basement with their father and they would laugh and shout and have a good ole time. I know he was fooling around with women the night before and that made him feel good in a different way than I can, I guess. I came here because I want help. I want my sweet husband back and I don't want any sexually transmitted disease.*

Jane's problem with her husband has a good chance of being worked through because his behavior only occurs when he is with his father and brothers, and not at other times. Resolving such a problem is more easily done when both recognize it as an issue and will work on it together. The reason that Jake acts differently when he is with the male members of his family than he does when he is alone with Jane will be uncovered when they are both in the office speaking to each other about it. This behavior looks as though it happens when he is with the male family members and not when he is away from them or with friends. This places him further along the *continuum* of outcomes, but the fact that it happens under these conditions makes it easier to resolve.

An Affair Within the Family

When a man finds his lover somewhere *in the family*, it is a grave attack on every family member—everyone suffers. Boundaries, the lines that keep us safe and secure, are crossed. Without respect for boundaries, anyone can go wherever he pleases. There are no limits. A stepdad can find his teenage or older stepdaughter attractive, and act on those thoughts. He may seek an affair with a sister-in-law or niece. Perhaps an affair well known to Americans is Woody Allen's affair with his wife's adopted daughter, Soon Yi Previn, who was more than thirty years younger than Allen.

Infidelity is always painful: No one is unscathed by it, from the oldest member to the youngest. When it happens within the family, it is not just an affair; it is a **toxic affair**. I say this with no intention of minimizing the pain of "regular" infidelity, but for the woman, a double betrayal of this type is excruciating.

Barbara and Robert

When I first saw Barbara, she was so disturbed that her story came out in bits and pieces between her tears. What she was trying to tell me was that she thought her husband, Robert, might be having an affair with her sister, Natalie. She said her sister openly flirted with him and he responded.

There was no evidence of Robert and Natalie's affair, but there was a history of her mother's two sisters having a serious problem in which one sister had an affair with the other's husband. The result was that the couple went off together. It was, of course, a family crisis, but it was more than something that happened in the past—it was a family story that carried enormous emotional weight to this day. Barbara may have been reacting to the past and making more of Robert and Natalie's suspected affair than it should be.

Barbara and I talked about the probability of them having an affair, and the actual evidence, but she felt she had to know for certain.

The Search for Truth

Barbara decided she must ask her husband if he was having an affair with Natalie. I worked with her on rehearsing it so she would be able to maintain control of her emotions as she asked what she wanted to know. Barbara did so, and found out that he was not having an affair and that he was aware of Natalie's flirting, but did not know how to handle it because he was afraid he would start trouble in the family. We talked about how boundaries are drawn verbally and by body language. Sometimes a lack of response can be the signal that is needed. In this case, Robert's nonresponse was interpreted by Natalie as permission to continue. So his plan was to be nice but not to respond to the flirting, and if this did not stop it, he and Barbara would speak to Natalie about it as a team. Since they both regarded Natalie as a difficult person, they would work with me on what they wanted to say and strategies for speaking with her without getting into an argument. This is a family in long-standing pain that should not be allowed to continue through the generations.

In some families like this, the members may try to hide what has happened. According to Murray Bowen, author of *Family Therapy in Clinical Practice*, some family members "emotionally cut off"; that is, they distance themselves from the family geographically and/or by cutting off communication. This does not work. Barbara's aunt (who had the affair) moved away with her sister's husband, received a divorce, and married her lover. Cutting off only creates a secret—a family secret that will eventually come out, as it did in Barbara's reaction. It is an indication of the degree of pain in the family. Barbara now can be the catalyst for change in the family by speaking about the hurt and letting her family talk about it and about those qualities that they love about their sister.

What Can You Do?

If you see infidelity present in either family, you may see women who look the other way and men who continue this behavior because it makes them feel "like a man." When you find yourself in a family in which affairs are encouraged by the men and silently suffered by the women, the situation has little chance of changing without some professional intervention so that both can understand the influence of family.

Checking into Infidelity

You must take many things into consideration before taking a stand, and the first one is your safety. If you have not talked to your husband or do not want to talk to him about his suspected or actual infidelity, you may choose to do so yourself or in the presence of a therapist. Before you confront him, you must be sure that he has not ever become physically abusive. A therapist will help him understand that his infidelity does not end when he gets out of bed with the woman, but it goes on to impact everyone—including the children, every day of their lives. Ideally, you should see a therapist together, but if he will not do that, *you must go alone*. Affairs do not just happen because of alcohol, the candlelight, or someone's father's tendency to have affairs. *An affair is a decision.*

Case Study: Counseling All Three in the Triangle

It is very unusual to counsel all three members of a triangle of infidelity, but this case provides information that you can learn from. The following story shows how each of the three individuals in this triangle were helped by therapy.

Jodi and Carter came in together because they had been having an affair for two months and Carter was very confused about his feelings. Jodi had been married for two years, divorced for four, and was a paralegal in the office where Carter, who was forty-five, was a lawyer. Carter felt that his marriage was not what he had imagined it would be. He felt that his wife, Arlene, was no longer as receptive to him as she had been. She seemed removed and was reluctant to talk about it.

Jodi was very attracted to Carter from the first time they met, and it was not long before they were sleeping together. She saw him every day at the office, but when she was home alone she texted him and waited for the next day to see him. Weekends were the hardest for Jodi because Carter was at home with Arlene and the boys. Jodi felt that Carter was too attached to his family. He talked about leaving them when he was with her, but he never took any steps to do so. When Jodi was angry about his inaction, she had sex with other men.

JODI: *They were not for a relationship but something to do because of my anger. I have a right as long as he goes home and sleeps with his wife.*

When I asked him if he did really want to leave, he hesitated and said he wasn't sure. Jodi became angry. Then he backtracked and said he did.

Carter was seen alone at the second session, which was set to review his feelings without Jodi present. Carter finally was able to say that he didn't know if he wanted to leave his marriage. He just wanted to change the atmosphere, but didn't know what to change or how. Then he changed his mind and said he wanted to be with Jodi. He clearly had work to do before he could make a decision. He told Jodi that he needed to sort out his issues with Arlene before proceeding with a decision. It was not the result Jodi had hoped for. She was disappointed and angry, but she agreed to it. Jodi was given a choice of a referral for therapy during this period.

Next, I met with Carter and Arlene. Arlene knew of the affair, but as was her way, she had kept quiet about it. Since this was the first time the affair was acknowledged by the two of them, the next few sessions were spent discussing it. Soon after that, Carter and Arlene worked on their family history, and from that many things became clear.

Their Marriage

Carter and Arlene met and dated in high school and married after graduation. Arlene worked the first nine years of their marriage as a bank teller so that Carter could go to college and law school. They moved to New York, where the college and law school were, and they continued living there after his graduation. Carter found a job at a law firm and they were busy buying a home and fixing it up. Arlene stayed at home to raise their three sons. The family did little together for fun. There were no vacations or dinners out. About this time, Carter started an affair with Jodi and told his wife about it a little later.

Arlene's Family History

Arlene said that her childhood had been difficult because her father was angry so much and she felt as though she had always been walking on eggshells. Her father was a carpenter and was frequently out of work. Her mother was a traditional homemaker with whom she got along very well. Arlene didn't want to set her father off because of his anger. Her mother was "long-suffering" and Arlene felt powerless as a child to help her. (Arlene was also long-suffering, as we shall see.)

ARLENE: *He left my mother and me three times for a period of months. I think he took off with his girlfriend. We knew he had one. We knew he had many. My mother was so frightened, but she tried to make our home nice for me. We celebrated the holidays by decorating the house, making gifts, and cooking special food together.*

Carter's Family History

Carter's father and mother had very little money. His father's work was seasonal and it was the lack of money that affected Carter's self-esteem and his desire to have a professional career. His father was depressed when he didn't work and full of daydreams when he did. His mother was very pleasant, but always frightened of what the financial future held for them. Carter had two brothers who left home early and, although they didn't attend college, they became successful in their work. They are not close, but do get together for Thanksgiving. They are attentive to their mother.

View of Their Marriage

Arlene's View

Arlene was like her mother, passive and nonassertive, but honest and loyal. She was pretty, but she knew that Jodi was a knockout, much prettier than she was. Arlene had not developed many interests. Sometimes she talked about going to college, but she never did. She said that they hadn't been able to afford it because her income was essential for Carter to attend college. She also said that she wanted to be a stay-at-home mom.

> ARLENE: *When we could afford to do more, I think I lost my self-esteem. I couldn't do anything.*

Most people who are abandoned in childhood, like Arlene, experience decreases in self-esteem at different periods in their lives. Arlene retreated from the world in a way and spent most of her time at home. She wasn't able to go to college. Most important, most women whose husbands have had an affair will experience a significant drop in self-esteem.

Jodi called a few times and Arlene became very upset. Even though Arlene didn't express her feelings much about the relationship with Jodi, she went to her internist and was placed on anti-anxiety medication. Carter did not know this until their joint meetings with me.

Carter's View

CARTER: *I was angry that Jodi called Arlene and said very mean things. For days, the boys wouldn't speak to me. I adore my children and this was very painful. She upset Arlene in a way I didn't know about. I believe I love Arlene, but it is our life I don't love. I married Arlene because I knew her from childhood through high school graduation, and she was a very stable person and she was pretty and sweet. I love her, but something is missing from our marriage. This is not what we worked for!*

Conclusions

Carter and Arlene had been so involved up to this time with the new marriage, school, the finances, the birth of the children, and buying and furnishing the new house that they hadn't realized something was wrong with their marriage. They have been together, but the intimacy in their marriage has decreased, and the passion needs to be regenerated. They both realize this now and will work together and in therapy to improve these areas.

The most obvious issue in Arlene's life is abandonment. Because her father abandoned the family three times during her childhood, the fear was always there. She feels that Carter's leaving his family to marry Jodi would be a repetition of her father's behavior, and it terrifies her. She knows that her marriage could end, but she believes that if she spoke of it, it could precipitate the ending. Once, when Carter did try to leave his family for Jodi, Arlene had a panic attack because she was re-experiencing abandonment. Carter had looked at it as a tantrum, but now realizes the basis of it and how hard it would have hit her.

Carter always wanted a close family and he consciously developed closeness with his children, who are very angry with him because of his behavior. He now realizes that Arlene has sacrificed much of her life for him, and he wants to stay and help her in her growth. He wants to support her in her college endeavor and any other interest she has.

Carter realizes that they now have money for vacations, dinner out, furnishing the house, and a new wardrobe for Arlene. They can live differently than when they were just married.

CARTER: *I am going to change my behavior. I've been blind!*

He is now aware that he has been self-centered and has ignored Arlene. Carter decided to end the relationship with Jodi and never start it again. He also realizes now that Jodi doesn't have any special interests either, but she is exciting because of her beauty and her glamorous way of dressing. His views have been superficial. Carter now wants to continue therapy with Arlene and begin to restructure their marriage.

Jodi's History

During my first meeting with Jodi, she described her father as sadistic, and Carter remembered that and correlated it to the mean messages she had sent Arlene. Jodi came to realize that the meanness in her treatment of Arlene was copied from her father's cold and uncaring behavior toward her and her mother. Jodi did mean things when she felt neglected or hurt. She had affairs in her first marriage, and she also went to bed with someone she hardly knew in order to hurt Carter because he did not leave Arlene. Jodi was very unhappy about this breakup, but will continue with her therapist. The rules have been set and she understands them. She will continue with her own therapy to recover from this situation and to learn from it.

The Impact of Their Family Histories

By looking at three generations, we are able to see the effect of previous generations and the effect on the younger generation. Now each person understands the reasoning behind their behavior. Therefore, they can feel less guilt and they can be more forgiving of themselves and the other person as they hear the whole story together.

Conduct a Generational Family History

Looking back on each person's generational family tree, you can see family events, behaviors, and traits that will show patterns. These patterns will bring you an understanding of your family and your husband's family and how their characteristics may influence the way each person behaves and how the couples interact. This is a very important exercise for your understanding of the degree of infidelity in family trees. Let little squares represent the men, and circles the women. Then connect them by lines. Instead of birth dates, look for behaviors in his family that may be indicative of generational infidelity. In your family tree, look for patterns and traits that show how you view infidelity and why. Then go through the family, collecting similar information until you see patterns of behaviors. Doing this allows you to be more aware, to discuss these patterns with your partner, and to keep them in mind in raising your children.

Exercise

Do a *family review* by asking yourself the following questions:

1. What was your family's belief about infidelity? What evidence do you have for this answer?
2. Were you aware of any infidelity in your family-of-origin? Yes/No
   If "Yes," did you see it in the extended family? Yes/No
   If "Yes," was it repeated in the next generations? Yes/No
3. If the answers have been "Yes," how did you react to it?
4. Was infidelity accepted by everyone?
5. What was considered being "manly" in your family?
6. How were women treated in your family?
7. Now, answer the same questions about your partner's family. Please write down any conclusions you can find from this family review of both families, just as was done with Arlene, Carter, and Jodi. What did you learn?
8. What conclusions can you draw about the attitudes and behavior of your family and your husband's?
9. What conclusions can you draw about how this has affected your marriage?

chapter six

LOSING SIGHT OF EACH OTHER

As we move along the continuum of reasons why men have affairs, the reasons become more serious. Now we will address those that can affect the tone of your home and your relationship, even for couples who have been happy for a long time. These changes are not like the transitions discussed in the previous chapter because they occur slowly, over time. Gradually, you find you have lost sight of each other. This is an unfortunate but correctable situation.

This situation can be seen in many ways—such as a lack of respect between the partners or poor communication—but more often appears as a loss of interest in one another. This shows a marriage that is hurting and may be in trouble. One or both partners seem lost to the other.

How Does This Situation Occur?

Often, people just seem to slide into a state of "losing sight of one another" because they don't address an issue, or don't know how to do so. They don't see a way out, and thus the tone may keep getting worse. When a couple begins to lose sight of one another, one of the first indications is that the tone in the home changes, as does the way you speak to each other. It is first important to understand *why* the tone has changed. Then, you can work to correct that. You must do this because when it occurs, the couple begins to speak harshly, rudely, and contemptuously to each other. For couples who have not spoken disrespectfully to one another before, such a change must be addressed.

Home is supposed to be our refuge, a haven against the elements, a place where we are welcomed and feel comfortable and where we can restore ourselves. But home can become a place where ongoing battles continue, where family members are juggling many problems, where expectations go unfulfilled, and where people speak harshly to one another. When this happens, home is not a haven, but hostile territory. When it is too hostile, it can become unbearable for its members, and the stress resulting from the atmosphere may cause one of the partners to have an affair. Such an affair is usually a fling, with no emotional attachment. As discussed in Chapter 1, flings are easier to resolve than are other types of affairs. Even so, the man's affair will affect the marriage, and his wife will expend much psychological energy coping with the aftermath of the infidelity.

In my experience as a therapist, transitions and the situations listed in this chapter are the most common reasons for affairs. Because so many affairs are due to couples having lost sight of each other, I want now to discuss five different couples and the actions they took to change the negative course they were on.

Children Taking Over

Couples who have active lives and busy children could be at risk for losing sight of each other. Even though they are busy because they are involved, supportive parents who are trying to do the right thing, they may be devoting too much of themselves to their children. The couple often has little time or energy to maintain a healthy connection of their own. This situation can occur if children are very young and need constant attention, or if the children are older and involved in various extracurricular activities.

How to Resolve It

At the first indication that this situation is happening, try to nip it in the bud. Couples need to connect, and there are many ways to do it. An easy way is to talk with your partner about how important it is to carve out time for just the two of you. Try an evening out for dinner or a movie. Keep in mind that it doesn't always need to be dinner with candlelight at an upscale restaurant. After the children are in bed, have a cup of coffee or a glass of wine and talk with each other. During this time, try to talk about something other than your children or stressful scheduling concerns. Save the issues that relate to the problems for "Talk Time," which is discussed at length in Chapter 11. (Talk Time is a special time set aside each week to discuss your issues so that they are contained and do not suddenly appear at any other times.) All other time together is designed for reconnecting after a busy day or week. Relax in whatever way works for you both—watch a movie, talk about a book you've read, go for a walk. If you played tennis or any other sport, try to find some time for that. One couple had a lot of fun when they bought a billiard table. When your anger dissipates, you can have friends join you. Balancing the hectic demands of parenthood with a healthy dose of couple time will go a long way toward keeping you in touch with each other. Later, in Part III, you will read about family meetings, which are intended for all the family to discuss how the family can work and play together.

Let's look at a couple who is struggling to make that connection.

Chris and Judy

Chris and Judy are a couple in their forties who made an appointment to see me because their family doctor suggested it. Judy suffers from migraines and is a chronic pain patient. They are parents of teenage boys who are now in the stressful process of applying to college. The boys are athletic and their lives revolve around sports.

> CHRIS: *Our house is bedlam. Things are just a mess and we can't seem to get order out of it. Our kids are teenagers and they never put their sports equipment away. Judy just can't cope with it. There is a lot of anger in our house and I'm not sure why. They all have hectic schedules. College applications are very stressful. We spend so much family time at meets and games that we never have any fun, not even on weekends. Everyone speaks in a nasty way to each other. I'm a phys ed teacher and I really love my job. Judy makes ceramics in a home studio that I built for her and she is very busy. Her work is admired and sells well.*

We talked more, and found that Chris and Judy threw themselves into trying to be the best parents possible, and in that process lost sight of each other. Judy started to talk of trips they never took:

> JUDY: *I don't mean European trips. I mean, getaway weekend trips would be all right. We never seem to go out together. He doesn't give me little gifts. We have grown apart and in a year the boys will be leaving. Then what do we have?*

That session ended with plans for Chris and Judy to have some time out together for dinners and family meetings to discuss some of the issues troubling them. The next two sessions were spent on issues of home organization, because Judy's mother had run a very organized home and Judy felt like a failure in comparison. The feeling between Chris and Judy was showing improvement. But it was not long before I received a call from Judy for an appointment because something "terrible" had come up. I saw they were both distressed when they came in.

JUDY: *I just found out. Chris told me that he had a one-night stand. Her name is Amy and she lives nearby.*

CHRIS: *I didn't plan it. It just happened. I just felt better talking with her. I called her weeks ago and told her Judy and I were now in therapy, working on our marriage and that I had made a mistake. I thought it would be better to clear the air.*

JUDY: *Do you love her?*

CHRIS: *No, I don't! I am never going to have any contact with her again. I am sorry. I wish I could turn time back. Please forgive me.*

Judy was very hurt by this. We now were going to help Judy recover from this affair. They both realized that they had lost sight of one another through the years, and that had affected each person. They had become argumentative and belligerent with each other, so much so that Chris sought another woman to talk with.

Chris and Judy knew they still loved each other, yet Chris had a brief fling. This was a wake-up call to both of them.

Conclusion

The first issue we worked on was Judy's feeling of betrayal, and restoring her self-esteem, which had dropped considerably. When Judy's emotions later calmed down, we addressed the reasons for the affair. Although we worked on their communication skills and other home management changes, they had to get back in touch with each other. It was important to them to make closer contact with each other and to bring romance back into their lives. Some of the exercises in Part III will help Judy and Chris communicate with care and teach them how to recognize the core of a message, so that they understand it, and can then express empathy to one another effectively.

When the atmosphere in this home first took on a persistent unpleasant tone, it was an indication of a problem. Problems need to be addressed as soon as possible so that they do not grow. Home management problems are somewhat common now that more women are working outside the home. Although working, raising children, taking them to all of their events, cleaning a home, and tending to the laundry are enormous tasks, a loving couple cannot allow themselves to lose sight of one another because of a hectic lifestyle.

No Time for Sex

Related to losing sight of each other is that many couples are having less sex than they used to. People are always concerned about how much sex they are having compared to others. They are distressed because they think that other couples have sex more frequently than they do. Actually, investigators have found that Americans have sex between one and three times a week. Younger couples have sex more frequently than older ones. The comprehensive and respected study, which was published in *Sex in America* (written by Robert Michael, John H. Gagnon, Edward O. Laumann, and Gina Kolata), examined the frequency of sex of both men and women for one year. The authors say, "We found that about 40 percent of married people have sex with their partner two or more times a week and well over half of people who are living together have partnered sex that often. Yet, fewer than a quarter of men and woman who are not living with a partner have sex that frequently. About half of all married people have sex with their spouses a few times a month."

Even though this is a common problem, lack of a healthy sex life can still have devastating effects on a marriage. Having a satisfactory sex life becomes difficult to accomplish and is usually the first thing to go when parents are exhausted and can't find the time for themselves or each other. Many married couples have slowly, over time, decreased their sexual time together until they may not be having any sex at all. The couple doesn't know how to solve the problem at home and they start blaming each other. Or, they blame themselves—women believe they are not attractive enough and men believe they are not sexual enough. It has a negative impact on both, and could even lead to an affair.

How to Resolve It

If you notice a decline in your sex life and would like it to change, look at your family's schedule and decide whether that is the problem. When you are angry with each other, excessively tired, or the tone in your home has taken a bad turn, it may be reflected in your sex life. If rearranging the schedule to free up some time doesn't bring change, you must look further.

Just as couples plan a trip to have fun, you must plan your life so that you are not exhausted and will have time for each other. To find this time, you may have to rearrange chores and priorities so that you are not too tired for each other. Believe it or not, these simple changes can make a big difference. From there, you can build to more intimate sessions until your sex life is restored.

COULD IT BE HORMONAL CHANGES?

Some of the causes for lack of desire may also include hormonal changes, such as those at perimenopause. The first step is to check with your internist, who may refer you to a gynecologist and your husband to a urologist. If there is no medical reason, the next step is to work with a therapist or a sex therapist. Lack of a sex drive is a common problem that can be solved through a variety of methods.

Noreen and Bob

Noreen and Bob came in for therapy because he was having an affair online. They were both employed, she in marketing and he in banking. They had three children who were very busy with their activities. The number of times they had sex dropped off to about once a month for longer than a year. At first, they made jokes about it, but it got worse and now it was down to zero. A few months earlier, Noreen's mother had become ill and required a great amount of Noreen's time. Noreen became so tired, she'd fall asleep as soon as her head touched the pillow, and the couple's sex life stayed at zero.

This is a time in their lives when time pressures, due to raising a family and work, become complicated by the life transition of caring for an ill parent. Bob found sexual time; however, it was with a woman he met in a chatroom. They never met in "real time." They worked out the three-hour time difference for their computer meetings, and Bob was feeling better about the lack of sex until Noreen woke one night and found that Bob was not in bed. She went to look for him and found him at the computer. It didn't take long for her to figure out what was happening. She made Bob send the woman a "good-bye" e-mail while she watched, and then put the woman's address in the blocked mail, so Bob would never receive her e-mail again—she hoped.

Although Bob loved Noreen, he wanted to have more sex and when it wasn't available at home, he reached out to someone else. Such problems can be solved when the basis of the relationship is good and people have the skills and are willing to try to use them. Noreen and Bob are just such a couple. They made an appointment to deal with the first issue, which was his Internet affair and Noreen's reactions.

As we moved on past the effects of the affair, Noreen and Bob made time for each other by scheduling a long weekend away. At first it seemed awkward, like a homework assignment, but the tensions soon disappeared and they began to relax with each other and have fun. Then they made love and cuddled. The next morning they had breakfast in bed and used their new skills in communication and problem-solving to find time to be with each other.

They started to communicate about the problem instead of ignoring it. When they stopped blaming each other and started looking for solutions, they found them. They investigated the benefits that Noreen's mother had under Medicare and were surprised and relieved to find help. They also supplemented this help with their own funds.

Boredom

One of the most common complaints of couples is that they are bored in their marriage. Often one partner feels that he or she has outgrown the other. Complaints sound like these:

- *I have left her behind.*
- *She doesn't show any interest in anything but the children.*
- *He is only interested in his business.*
- *She has nothing to say.*
- *At dinnertime, we turn on the TV or else the silence would be deafening.*

Again, this can happen to people because they are so busy and so much is expected of both husband and wife in the age in which we live. In simpler times before MBAs, the BlackBerry, two-family incomes, and the Internet, families had more time to spend together—to take classes, to develop hobbies, and to explore their interests. Now just a child's application for college can cause paralysis in the family because of deadlines and the time needed to see that kids do everything they need to do to look good on their application.

People can stop growing intellectually and personally when they are caught up in all the roles they have assumed. They find that they have little to say to each other and they become resentful and bored with their marriage. When this happens, they lose their attractiveness to one another because they find life with the other is boring—and one or both may have an affair.

How to Resolve It

If this is the case in your relationship, ask yourself how you two have grown as a couple over the years. Have you made new friends, found new hobbies, or expanded your horizons in any way? If you haven't, you may have lost sight of each other and what you could do as a couple. Then you suddenly realize you could be bored in your marriage. Having made that discovery, you can look toward ways to make changes in your lives. Think back to things that you used to enjoy or activities you wanted to pursue, or look in the local papers for what is going on and what you can participate in. Ask others; there are film groups, hiking groups, astronomy groups—groups for just about any interest. By learning something new and fun together, you will remind each other of your intellect, your passion, and your depth as individuals, and you will make new friends.

Boredom, however, is not the only reason why people lose sight of one another. Over the years, couples change. They must not ignore the changes or they may find themselves going in different directions, as our next couple has.

Betsy and John

Betsy came for counseling because she was depressed. She and John were approaching their fifteenth wedding anniversary and she didn't feel like planning any celebration.

BETSY: *My mother told me to start planning something and she would help, but as I started talking with her, I began to cry and once I started, I thought I would never stop. That was the beginning of a few steps that led me here to your office. John doesn't want to come, so I think it may be worse than I believe, if that's even possible. I think John would rather get a divorce than celebrate and when I asked him that, he was very quiet. He said things that were almost unbearable to hear, like I was boring, I didn't grow, I am not the same person he married. It sounded as though we had grown apart.*

Just then, there was a knock on the door. It was John.

JOHN: *Betsy told me she would be here and I could come. I wasn't going to, until I realized how far things have gone.*

This was a lucky turn of events, because many husbands do not want to come for therapy. Sometimes they change their minds, as John did, when he realized the extent of the unhappiness he felt about his marriage and that the situation was serious.

It came out that he was very attracted to someone he worked with and that they have dinners together even when they really don't have to for work. Her name was Kate. She was manager of a new division, and was important to developing the marketing project that was under way.

JOHN [with enthusiasm]: *She is a whiz—sharp as a tack! It is exhilarating to be with....*

John's voice dropped off as he realized what he was saying, and Betsy was in tears. I realized that John was having an emotional affair with his colleague at work. Betsy said, *I guess the class mother and Scout leader can't compare to her.* John tried to tell Betsy that they haven't grown as a couple.

Conclusion

This was the beginning of considerable confessions, tears, and promises to make changes from each one. Up until now, they had swept the problem under the rug. John agreed to stay in therapy and to stop his emotional affair. Together, we set the rules for John's interactions with Kate—since they continue to work together, it was to be professional, and all their interactions were to be described to Betsy.

He also told Betsy that he loved her, but he wanted things to change in their lives. In the next few sessions, the couple dealt with the pain of the emotional affair, began the process of setting goals for themselves and for their marriage, and worked on ways to meet them. Betsy received support for the projects she wanted to explore. It took quite a few sessions to cope with the hurt, but Betsy began to explore the world and her own talents. After a rocky start, they did very well, once they started talking.

An Unavailable Partner

Long separations can have a negative impact on couples, causing them to lose sight of one another because they are literally out of each other's sight! Sometimes these separations are due to work schedules that require one of the partners to work out of town for a year, maybe even at a research project in another country, or at desolate places like the South Pole, or duty on a submarine. Perhaps the most difficult separations are those that occur when a loved one is in a war zone.

In all lengthy separations, the spouse at home becomes both mother and father to the children. He or she takes over all the responsibility and handles all emergencies alone, while the one not there misses out on the developmental changes of the children and all of their special events like plays, Little League games, and graduations. The tone of the home changes: Aside from the enormous reordering of the daily life of both, each is very lonely.

Most stressful for both is the terrible danger a military spouse is in by living and working in harm's way. Such stresses can contribute to infidelity in a family, even though the married couple love each other.

How to Resolve It

Couples in these situations face an extra challenge in solving their problem, because they are so far away from one another. They could each seek out support groups, which are very helpful to those coping with difficult life problems like infidelity. In a group, the members find support and not criticism. Members benefit from the experience of others and the camaraderie of feeling they are not alone. The newer members of the group see that others in the group were once where they are now, and that they have made progress in handling their issues. Those who have been in the group for a while can see the progress they have made compared to the newer members. In addition, they receive support, advice, and friendship. This is helpful for everyone involved.

Jocelyn and Lewis

The previous couples have been dealing with day-to-day life and the changes they have been experiencing in their lives. Yet the most difficult circumstances can occur when the partners are not living under the same roof.

Jocelyn and Lewis were married five years when he was called up by the Army Reserve to serve in Iraq. With two little children and no family nearby, Jocelyn was very anxious or, as she put it, "spooked."

JOCELYN: *I was always worried about Lewis. His mother was a widow and she called me for reassurance every other day. My parents lived outside of Portland and they called and were supportive. But it was hard; I felt lonely. Money was a constant problem, so we had to limit recreational activities. I love the children, but I needed a break. Finally, I was able to get some space. I joined a support group for other partners and they offered child care. Other things began to improve. I developed friends. We had potluck get-togethers. We had group activities where we made Christmas presents for the kids. Those of us who had no plans for Thanksgiving had a holiday dinner together. It is amazing what can happen when people get together to help each other.*

Then two things happened that really caused us a depression as a group. Some of the men and women were given a second deployment and one guy asked his wife for a divorce because he fell in love with another GI, his sergeant. I didn't think that was allowed, but he was going to marry her. We, then, felt like the whole thing was falling apart. Then some news hit me personally. Lewis told me near the end of his second deployment that he was having an affair with a woman in the captain's office and he wanted a divorce. He also wanted to plan out our separation before he got home.

The independence that Jocelyn had achieved during those years prepared her to fight this.

JOCELYN: *This was not like Lewis. He was the poster boy for the good American: fair, likable, and one who always stood shoulders above everyone else.*

Without knowing what else to do, Jocelyn found the e-mail and phone number of the chaplain with Lewis's unit, and after a number of conversations, the chaplain asked Lewis to come in to talk with him. Lewis then became a member of a group of reserves who were in some way involved with infidelity while they were also fighting a very dangerous war. These soldiers feel the stress minute by minute in a country where they can't relate to anything, and nothing seems real.

Conclusion
Months later in a letter to Jocelyn, Lewis apologized and addressed her hurt. He told her what the situation was like:

LEWIS: *My world consisted of the ground thirty feet around me that could have IEDs or a car bomb. I feel badly. I lost all perspective of what was important to me. You and our little boys are most important. I will not see her again, and I will try every day of my life to make this up to you.*

Serving one's country in wartime is a stressful experience and as a result, people do things they might never do otherwise. Couples who care for each other can find themselves in circumstances like military deployment or unaccustomed lifestyles that change the tone of their life together. They need to be analytical, that is, step back and see the situation as it truly is, understanding that the circumstances are not normal, but temporary. Don't make any big decisions under such conditions. Find the help you can until the situation changes.

Bereavement
Individuals dealing with grief often are so shaken by the trauma of loss that they lose touch with their partner. They may be melancholy and introverted, or they may begin acting completely out of character. Normally, the death of a loved one is a transition, and one that we must adjust to and make part of our life. All loved ones must adjust to a family loss, but there are times when the resolution does not proceed as expected. So it changes character and may change the atmosphere in the home. There are many who are not able to move on from

bereavement and join in the family activities because they are weighed down by the heaviness always present in their heart.

Dr. Virginia A. Simpson, founder of the Mourning Star Center (which according to its mission statement "provides loving support in a safe place where grieving children can share their experience as they move through their healing process") and the executive counseling director for funeral homes throughout the United States and Canada, is a leading expert on bereavement. She wrote, "Grief becomes complicated when the reactions that would be considered normal become chronic and persistent, and interfere with daily life and relationships. When a parent or spouse's grief becomes focused on the loss to the exclusion of maintaining good relations, the people within the living family come to feel as though their lives have less meaning than the person who died, and this can result in serious conflict within the family system."

Clearly, grief that continues can be so disruptive to a family that one member may act out against it in ways that are unusual for him—including having an affair.

How to Resolve It

If darkness comes over a bereaved person for a long period of time and does not lift, he or she must be helped with their grieving. When grief continues for a longer-than-expected time, the bereaved one should seek counseling. Other family members may need counseling as well.

In all of the previous case studies, the couples were able to communicate with each other, to talk over their issues, and had the means to come to a resolution. The next study is different, in that the reaction to the death of a loved one is causing tension in the tone of the home.

Jack and Liz

Jack and Liz came to therapy because Jack would leave the house in the evenings to go out and get a drink at the neighborhood bar. Liz thought that he might be having an affair. Liz's reaction, however, was blunt and not as strong as others who have come to the office with such a problem.

> JACK: *I am not having an affair. I go out for some drinks because I am beginning to feel depressed in our home. Liz doesn't talk. She either lies down or watches TV. I have thought of having an affair because I can't stand what has happened to us since her sister, Victoria, died, but I won't. Liz needs to talk to someone.*

This is at the core of the problem that Jack and Liz came in to talk about. Jack is not having an affair; he is running away from his "home of grief," as he put it. Liz's depression started after the death of her identical twin sister, Victoria, four years ago. She and her sister had been very close and she talked of twin stories, which showed them to be on the "same wavelength and telepathic," to explain their closeness. Dr. Simpson writes, "Every relationship we have reflects back to us parts of who we are and we have to learn to find ourselves without that reflection."

> JACK: *Liz's life practically stopped when her sister died. She acted as though her life ended and that she was the one who died, if that makes sense to you. I did everything I could for her. Our whole life was over when Victoria died.*

Jack and Liz's children reacted more to the loss they felt from their mother's lack of involvement in their lives than to their aunt's death. Jack's need for companionship and to stop living in a house filled with grief led to his affair.

Conclusion
When grief goes on for a long time, the grieving individual can be helped by memorializing the loved one in an appropriate manner. For example, grief began to shift with Liz when she started some personal projects. She started small: The first was a memory book for Victoria's children. The thoughts that came to Liz while working on

this project were subsequently discussed in our therapy sessions. Some old pain came up, as did wonderful memories. This balance helped Liz remember Victoria as a person, not as a saint. It was freeing for her to talk about the problems they had as sisters, as well as the happy times. When we had reached this step, we began thinking of a project that could memorialize her sister. Since her sister loved needlework, Liz started a group that provided needle art materials to teenagers in lower-income neighborhoods. She got funding from local businesses and found other women to help. At Christmas, they sold their work at a local fair. Liz is busy now trying to develop this idea and present it to other groups. She continued in individual therapy to understand her long period of unresolved grief and also in couples therapy to reconstruct her marriage. The outcome for this family was good.

Exercise

1. Have you noticed a change in tone in your home during the past few years? Yes/No
2. If "Yes," would you describe it as any of those discussed?
   Children Taking Over: Yes/No
   No Sex: Yes/No
   Boredom: Yes/No
   Unavailable Spouse: Yes/No
   Bereavement: Yes/No
   Other:
3. Which of the following would help you?
   Better Communication: Yes/No
   Spend More Time Together: Yes/No
   Prioritize Scheduling and Eliminate Unnecessary Things: Yes/No
   Manage Home Better: Yes/No
   Check Community Services for Help: Yes/No
   Check Government Services for Help: Yes/No
   Therapy: Yes/No
   Other:

chapter seven

CHANGING EXPECTATIONS

We are moving along the continuum to affairs that put the marriage on shaky ground. Up to this point, the reasons for the affair have been problems that have solutions, such as a plan for reconnection, a promise to change, or continued therapy for a particular issue. In the category discussed in this chapter, some of these reasons for affairs may mean the end of the marriage, while others may come close. You must think through the answer for yourself without making hasty conclusions. *Throughout this book there is hope that couples can recover from their various issues, and survive—but if not, the belief is that the individuals will recover.*

A common thread in all of these affairs is that a key expectation has not been communicated to the other, has not been known or understood. We will start with the most common reason, which is that one member of a couple becomes disappointed in his partner because his expectations have not been met.

Unfulfilled Expectations

When couples marry, they have certain expectations of each other. According to Dr. Clifford Sager, in his work on marriage contracts and the expectations of the couple, some brides and grooms talk about their expectations; others aren't verbalized but are understood by each; and some are beyond their consciousness', that is not known by either. These expectations are based on what they see in their partner, their parents, the family roles, and the rules that guide them and the world around them. Most important, however, they are formed from their own desires and needs.

Many people come to therapy because of unfulfilled expectations. These are a few examples:

- A man may silently expect to become a big-time moneymaker, but he turns out to be a salaried man and is stressed by not meeting his own expectations.
- The husband may expect that the wife will be very interested in sex, but after a few years, this disappears.

- The couple is arguing because the wife had not realized that she secretly wanted her husband to change his religion to hers, and he does not want to do that.
- A quiet person who marries the "take-charge guy" may in time seem too quiet. He then becomes annoyed with her, while she sees him as a controller. He no longer helps her—he dictates to her.
- A superorganized woman may marry the "spur of the moment" guy because he seems like so much fun to be with—only to find he is *too* spontaneous and she wants to have more plans and details. When she asks for this, he finds her to be overbearing.
- The Beauty may marry Mr. Wonderful, only he finds she is very self-centered and he is angry because she doesn't much notice him. In other words, they are both so involved with their own beauty (which attracted them to each other) that they don't give back the adoration they were expecting from the other.
- A woman may expect her husband to provide financial security, and somewhere along the line he feels he is overburdened. Maybe his father has a heart attack and he decides that he must get out of "the rat race" before he too becomes sick, and so they will have a less upscale lifestyle. She doesn't want to give up the country club, the opera and theater tickets, the foreign travel, or move to a smaller home. She becomes angry, and the tone of their relationship changes.
- The woman who manages money well marries the man who is an Adonis, and finds that the Adonis spends too much money on clothes and she must control the spending. So she becomes domineering in his eyes.

These are situations in which two people marry with expectations, but their virtues become the vice. These disappointments begin to show up in the couples' interactions. The expectations that are not realized can cause problems because they do not get discussed. Some people may feel so disappointed in their marriage that they look somewhere else for someone with the quality they desire.

"Wants" Versus Core Values

All of us live with values that can be negotiated and some that cannot. Dr. Murray Bowen defined a person's core self as made up of both types. The non-negotiable values are our *solid self* and cannot be changed, and no amount of discussion, persuasion, or coercion will alter those beliefs. The preceding example of the husband who does not want to change his religion may illustrate one such value. The values that can be changed are part of the *pseudo-self*.

How to Solve the Problem

Unfulfilled expectations do not necessarily spell the end of a relationship, but they must be addressed and accepted. These are the expectations that Sager has indicated are beyond our awareness. Therefore, to find out what these expectations mean to an individual, the couple must have an honest discussion. For example, the woman who must have a lavish lifestyle may have a background of poverty and deprivation that is unimaginable to her husband, one so terrible that she has kept it hidden. That may be a problem that can be worked through when effective communication is used.

Some core issues or values, such as wanting to have children, may be unfixable. These expectations are non-negotiable for some, so their expectations cannot change. In these cases, unfulfilled expectations may mean that the two partners are no longer compatible in some vital way.

Beth and Joshua

Beth and Joshua met on a college expedition to an archeological dig in Israel, where they both had a wonderful time. As a couple, they traveled the country and toured as many neighboring countries as they could. During the year after that, they saw each other often before graduation. Then Joshua went to graduate school in New England, and Beth in New York. Both made frequent trips to visit each other. After graduation, Joshua got a job on a research team, and Beth worked for a television news network as an assistant producer. They felt fortunate that they both were hired by firms in the same city,

Atlanta. They made a commitment to each other that they would always be together, and agreed to make decisions that would honor that commitment. That was the extent of what they said about their expectations for their future together.

They were like many of today's young generation who are excited about their careers. Beth was moving up at the network and was given increasingly more responsibility. She put in long hours, and traveled to many places to work on stories. Joshua was left alone, and more and more he began to realize that this wasn't the life he wanted.

One day, when Beth came home from a trip to Dubai, Joshua surprised her with tickets for a long weekend at Hilton Head, where they could relax and enjoy themselves in the water and at the beach. She was delighted. It was just the kind of vacation she loved. On the second day of their holiday, Joshua said he wanted to talk to her about something.

JOSHUA: *I know our careers are going well, but what about children? We can't wait too long.*
BETH: *We never talked about kids.*
JOSHUA: *I thought we had. You love my nieces and nephews. We have all these great get-togethers.*
BETH: *I do love them. But I'm on such a roll with my career. I don't know what to say.*
JOSHUA: *Beth, if you get pregnant, they can't fire you. There are laws against that.*
BETH: *Yes, but I won't get any of the good assignments anymore.*
JOSHUA: *Don't you want children?*
BETH: *I don't know. I don't not want them, but I'm not excited about them. I want the kind of life we had in college. Not being torn between work and children.*

So they decided to put off the discussion for six months. No definite conclusion was reached. As the decision continued to be put off, Joshua became more and more depressed. He started telling his problems to his coworker, Leah. They would have dinner together on the nights when Beth worked late. As their relationship developed, Joshua felt very close to her, and they began sleeping together.

Joshua and Beth came in for therapy after he told her that he was attracted to Leah and was sleeping with her. Beth was very upset.

BETH: *So it's my job or a baby?*
JOSHUA: *Why can't it be both? Your job and a baby.*
BETH: *I don't want a baby.*
JOSHUA: *Why didn't you tell me that sooner?*
BETH: *I never knew it was so important.*
JOSHUA: *You saw my family—all the kids. I thought you would understand.*
BETH: *You saw my family—I'm the oldest of eight children. I had to work, work, and work. I don't want that again. I thought you were a career guy and wanted the same for me.*

Joshua and Beth had not verbalized their desires for the life they wanted together, so they had expectations that went unfulfilled. Joshua cheated on Beth by having an affair with Leah, rather than really discussing their problem further. We spent time helping Beth with her feelings about the affair.

Conclusion

The shock of the affair caused Joshua and Beth to talk about their different expectations for their future together. After hours of discussion, they could not come to a compromise. Neither one could give up on their expectations. They were intelligent people who loved each other, but both found the expectations of the other unacceptable. Their therapy goal changed to helping them separate. They did not separate in anger; they said appreciative things to each other and they reviewed every way they could possibly make it work. At their last session together, they gave each other a gift that had special meaning for them and each wrote a letter to the other. Writing the letters was therapeutic and provided something they could keep and read when needed. Their breakup was sad, but it was a separation that had meaning, not bitterness.

Retaliation

Couples who have been disagreeing with each other for some time are often angry. One of the least effective and most destructive ways to cope with anger is by having an affair in retaliation for some hurt. Yet this is somewhat common. Retaliation affairs are an expression of rage at the partner. They can be a result of knowing the partner had an affair or multiple affairs. Other reasons relate to years of mistreatment that ate away at the person's core values. The person who retaliates is for some reason feeling too angry from living with an emotionally abusive spouse, or feels powerless in his marriage to act in a more assertive way, so he resorts to a very destructive way: an affair. Such an affair could be a way of getting back for other hurts, but in any case it makes a statement—a statement about anger, pain, and powerlessness. Retaliation affairs can complicate life and create many more problems than were there to begin with.

How to Avoid Retaliation

Some couples face infidelity based on retaliation because they do not have good communication skills. Because they aren't able to speak with each other personally and intimately, they can't find out what the problem is, how the other is feeling, or what they want from one another. Their marriage could be richer and grow in intimacy if they could effectively speak with one another. If they keep their problems to themselves and do not even approach one another because they know an argument would ensue, they are only increasing the distance between them. Effective communication skills help a couple to problem-solve without the negativity that may have hampered any previous attempts. Most people react positively to being spoken to with respect and being shown empathy, which is the aim of good communication. Reacting with retaliation shows an out-of-control person. His anger must be understood, but you must tread carefully and with help because you do not know what behavior such a person is capable of. If this is your problem with your partner, first see a therapist alone so that he can give you an idea of the degree of anger and guide you and your husband through this process. At that point, you can use many of the self-help skills in this book.

Sophie and Ted

Sophie and Ted, who had been married thirty years, came into my office because Ted had an affair with a woman they both knew. It was not long before a more complete, but complicated, story came out: They had *both* had affairs.

Sophie had an affair first, and then Ted had one to retaliate for Sophie's affair (which was with her dentist, Dr. Harris). At that time, Sophie had been very worried about her marriage to Ted, thinking he was overinvolved with work, and that they spent very little time together. At one of her dental appointments, Dr. Harris asked how she was, and as she talked she started to cry so badly that he was concerned for her and started to talk with her. He was very comforting and supportive, and he provided the attention that she needed. He continued his support through talks with her outside of the office. Then they started meeting for lunch, after work, and on weekends. Soon, they were in bed together. Ted found out about their relationship because of some confusion in the dentist's bill and he "hit the ceiling," as he put it. He threatened to report the dentist to the licensing bureau. Ted's anger seemed to know no bounds. Dr. Harris had a change of heart and refused to see Sophie privately and also suddenly had no dental appointments available for her.

Ted's anger increased until he felt he had to get even, which he did by having a brief affair, and then telling Sophie about it as soon as he could. Sophie was devastated, and eventually she and Ted made an appointment with me to sort things out.

Both affairs hurt and caused pain. Ted wanted Sophie to know how much her affair hurt him, so he saw to it that she experienced the pain the other partner feels. This did not solve their problem, but instead worsened it to the point that the marriage was on shaky ground.

Conclusion

In our work together, we started from the beginning and found that Ted and Sophie were a couple who had lost sight of one another and ignored the situation until they were in a crisis. Their life had become routine to the point that they hardly spoke to each other. Both affairs were flings, not romantic love affairs, and they were easy for them to end. Ted loved Sophie and wanted the two of them to breathe new life into their marriage. The most significant problem was that both felt their marriage was in trouble, but neither spoke to the other about it or did anything constructive that would have started them on the way to finding out what was wrong and what could be done. Fortunately, marital problems like these are not as difficult as others to resolve.

People have affairs to retaliate when they are angry. Underlying the anger are other emotions. The main one is a feeling of powerlessness; the second is pain. In this case, Ted felt powerless about his wife having an affair; and his first reaction was to strike back. When a husband has an affair because he feels powerless, the couple must get to the bottom of his feelings.

The anger was so great that they wanted a trial separation. They set up rules governing how this would happen in terms of seeing each other and not seeing others. Both continued coming to therapy to review the affairs and the nonrecognition of each other's needs. Things improved and Ted moved back home. They continued meeting with me until they became a couple that communicated well, and they celebrated the end of their problems with a weekend getaway.

Attention

Closely related to the retaliation affair is one that is caused by the need for attention. The motivation for this affair is different from the retaliation affair. In this situation, the husband has an affair because he cannot get his wife to give up a certain behavior or to do something he wants. He also feels angry at covering up his feeling of powerlessness. These husbands, and probably their wives as well, can't talk about or acknowledge that there is a problem in the marriage. So the husband (although it may also be the wife) has an affair and soon after lets the spouse know about it.

How to Manage These Situations

This chapter is about expectations that couples have or assume they should have. In such relationships, you must validate yourself. This is being clear on your rights as an individual and making "I" statements about who you are and what you will and won't do. You will learn more about this in Part III, but the following is an **"I" statement.** *I will not change plans with my mother when she has been wanting me to take her out for a day for such a long time. If we can't get a sitter, you will have to stay home or we will have to make a compromise, but seeing my mother must be part of that.*

This woman's solid self or core value was that her elderly mother needed some time out of the nursing home.

Georgia and Miles

Georgia and Miles came into the office because of an affair Miles had with Cathy, a family friend. Cathy was married to Rick. They all were in the same neighborhood social group. When there is an affair like this "among friends," the emotions are compounded not only by the affair, but by the betrayal of friendship. Georgia felt betrayed by Cathy, whom she had considered her best friend since they had moved to their new beachfront neighborhood, as well as betrayed by her husband. An affair draws an enormous reaction, but when it is with a woman the wife knows, it is a double betrayal.

Like most cases of infidelity, Georgia's recovery from his affair required as much attention to her emotional state as to the marriage. Miles was very remorseful. He felt shut out of Georgia's life. They had moved Georgia's ailing elder mother into a small guesthouse on their property, and Georgia was very busy taking care of her. By the time Miles came home at night, she was exhausted. Although Miles helped, Georgia insisted that she spend hours sitting with her mother. The lifestyle they had envisioned when they bought their beach home did not materialize, and Miles felt very much alone.

MILES: *Moving to the beach was a great opportunity for us, but Georgia couldn't enjoy it and was unmovable about finding some supplementary care for her mother. I recognized what I did was wrong—was terrible. I don't know what I was thinking, but I was so sorry. I know we could have had a wonderful life in this beach house. It was summer and the kids were away at camp.*

Georgia and Miles finally opened up with each other. Georgia told Miles that her mother had spent the first eight years of her life in an orphanage, and Georgia could not bear thinking of her mother being alone while they went out. It was too much like the orphanage.

MILES: *How can that be like the orphanage? She has a big ocean-view home with anything that she could want. We are usually in the neighborhood, just a phone call away. We taught her how to dial 911 and number 1 for us on the speed dial. Georgia, you are making this harder than it has to be. I am so desperate to enjoy what I worked so hard for with you. Why can't we? What can I do?*

Conclusion

This was the beginning of their working through this issue. Often the problem is not insolvable: Communication may be the real issue. If one speaks with the other about what is really on his mind and the other listens, there would be no reason for an affair caused by the need for attention.

Making an Exit

The first three affairs discussed in this chapter have a lot in common. One individual, at least, of the couple feels anger because he is powerless to effect change about an important issue in his relationship. The first case concerns a value question upon which the partner cannot compromise and which was not communicated to the other early in their relationship. In the others, *communication* is at the bottom of solving their issues.

There are some situations, however, in which anger and powerlessness are not part of the picture, because one spouse has made a decision to leave the marriage without discussing it with the other. We will look at these more difficult cases now.

Making an exit occurs when one person decides to have an affair as a way of leaving the marriage. The "other woman" is often caught up in this drama. She doesn't realize that she is being used by a man who wants to end his marriage, but has no intention of marrying her. He either tells his wife of the affair or leaves clues. After she discovers the affair, he either leaves or starts therapy with her. It is not long after therapy begins that it becomes obvious he is not in therapy to work through the issues of the affair, but to help him leave.

Therapy time must be spent on her recovery, as well. Some men know this will happen, and the affair and subsequent counseling is a way to end the marriage and to be sure that the wife's emotional needs are attended to. Part of his agenda is that the therapist will tend to his wife's emotional health. Having a therapist "take care of his wife" makes him feel less guilty about leaving her.

Individuals who see a therapist even though they plan to leave the marriage may also do this because of some ambivalence about leaving, an inability to address difficult topics, or issues about abandonment. Before a marriage ends, it is important for both to understand why, just as it is with every affair.

"We broke up because he had an affair" is not a satisfactory answer. It's harder to start over when one doesn't know why the affair occurred. Remember, an affair is a *maladaptive response* to a problem in the marriage or with one or both of the individuals in the marriage. It may be possible to prevent a breakup if the reason is understood, but the man involved in an exit affair is a planner and may not change his mind easily.

How to Deal with an Exit Affair

If your partner has had an exit affair and has already made the decision to end your relationship, your most important task is to understand why he wants to leave. You will be obsessing about this for a long while afterward. It would be easier if he would come to therapy with you so that you can hear it from him in the presence of a professional. If he doesn't, you must ask for time with him so that he can explain this decision to you. It is your right to have such an explanation. You should have the opportunity to ask your partner questions, an opportunity that you probably won't have again. You should continue with your therapist because you need help in getting through the pain and the grieving process, and you will need guidance in your obsessive thinking (see Chapter 11), so you can start to rebuild your life. Whenever a marriage or relationship ends, it is imperative to understand why it did; it will help you in working through this loss and in future relationships that you may have.

Lorrie and Ricky

Many years ago, Lorrie and Ricky came into my office because Ricky was having an affair. They were a couple who had grown very far apart. Ricky moved out first, and when that was done, he told Lorrie about the affair. Then he made an appointment to see me. The glue in their marriage had been the excitement of the hippie movement, but that was years ago. They had worked together on civil rights, had many hippie friends, and there had been great excitement in their lives. This is a phenomenon that happens with couples—when the excitement of working on a project, movement, or cause ends, they find that something is missing, something that flourished during the excitement they had drawn from their activities together.

Ricky bought and decorated a condo and was active in the condo community. He would get up early and run laps, and he played tennis daily. When he came to the office I could see he was trim and in good physical shape, and he wore a color-coordinated tennis outfit. Lorrie arrived separately and was dressed in a dark, full dress, designed to cover her obese figure. Her legs were swollen and she walked with difficulty, using a cane.

Ricky had already established himself in a different lifestyle, one that she could not fit into. She had also established herself in her own lifestyle, an intellectual one that included concert-going, poetry readings, and museum fundraising.

Their early years, however, were very different.

LORRIE: *Those were great years. Then we had children and settled down, and the fun disappeared. I guess it happened slowly. I gained weight. I became interested in community events. I went to fundraisers. Ricky never wanted to go. I changed. I know I gained a great deal of weight. My legs are so swollen I can hardly walk.*

RICKY: *I think we were great hippie partners, but couldn't make the change. I like swimming and playing tennis. I've done well in my business and now I work part-time. I can't go back to "what was." We just aren't hippies anymore.*

This was typical of *making an exit*. The husband makes the decision to leave and may actually have taken those steps, as Ricky did. He needed an affair to help him ease out of the marriage and maybe to bring the spouse to a therapist to help her in her recovery. Some men have an affair to see how it would feel to have another relationship, and then they leave. Of course, an affair will not give him the answer. They have the affair and then consider the end of the marriage a fait accompli. In this case, Ricky had definitely made that decision, so my role was to help Lorrie recover and find a new life for herself.

Conclusion

Ricky felt like a "new man with a new life" and he would not change his mind. What he would do was to come for joint counseling to make the separation smoother and to be sure that they took the steps to introduce the children to what was happening, and to continue to show them he was part of their lives. After this phase was complete, I continued to help Lorrie, who wanted to continue her charity work. When someone has decided to make an exit from his marriage and he won't try to solve the problems, you must understand why for your own information. Then you must build your new life, which can be what you want it to be. For example, Lorrie had interests, support groups, and involvement in community organizations already in place. In the same way, you may find that you like many things from your new life more than the old one.

An Old Flame

Therapists are hearing of more "old flame" affairs in recent years because of the Internet. With the advent of this digital marvel, more and more people can find each other than ever before. There was a time when, after graduation day, you knew you might never see your fellow graduates again, or at least infrequently, maybe at the class reunions. Now, however, people are finding "lost" friends on the Internet all the time. They Google them or find them on Facebook or one of the many search engines on the Internet. School reunions use the Internet to send out messages and e-mail addresses, so that more people can maintain contact with each other.

Along with these reconnections comes the rekindling of old flames. Contacting an old flame takes the former couple back to years past, to their history together. That history most likely was a happy one, occurring at a time when they were younger, but it skipped over later years—some that may have been more troubled. It is often not fair to compare married life to a past "young love," which for some may be more fantasy and projection than reality-based. When old flames meet again, they transport themselves back to the early stage of love, where passion is high. This may not compare well to their present marriages, where passion may have declined. Passion is that state of intoxication in which everything feels wonderful, like Gene Kelly dancing joyously in *Singing in the Rain*. Going back to another carefree time in life may blind a person to the realities of the present situation.

Many people leave their spouses to marry an old flame. Dr. Nancy Kalish, a clinical psychologist, has been doing research and writing on this topic for nearly twenty years. In her ten-year study of nearly 2,000 couples, the lost-love marriages, which began as affairs, do very well. The individuals have no remorse for leaving their previous marriage, and the divorce rate is 1.5 percent, compared to the national figure of near 60 percent. However, Kalish writes that many gave up custody of their children, moved to other states, and lost businesses and friendships. They realize that they have hurt innocent spouses and children. She writes on her website: "Reunions between married 'old flames' are not nearly as successful as reunions between single, divorced or widowed former sweethearts."

In part, the appeal of affairs with old flames may be the excitement of new romance compared to old, but most likely it may be that the marriage of the man who is searching is already on shaky ground. Stories that therapists hear in their offices tell of men and women using the Internet to search out old flames when things are not going well in their marriage. This is another example of a *maladapted solution* to an existing problem.

How to Deal with Old Flames

Most people look online out of curiosity to see what others are doing, but when they find an old flame, curiosity changes to interest. Simon, like others who have renewed contact with the old flame, found himself going back emotionally many years to a younger age. He again experienced passion, one part of the leg of the triangle of true love. Passion and fantasy make a powerful combination. He is not thinking rationally like Barry did in the group of long-term married couples who talked of affairs (Chapter 5).

If this is the kind of affair that has occurred in your marriage, you need to allow time for your husband to process what has happened. I believe you must find a therapist whom you see as a couple and individually. This situation is very difficult, and you must gather support and do whatever will be self-nurturing for you.

Joann and Simon

Simon remembers the nervousness he felt as he entered the downtown hotel in Baltimore, which he hadn't visited since high school. He was there to meet Joann, his high school girlfriend, at the restaurant. They hadn't seen each other since college. There had been an article in the local newspaper about her, with her e-mail address listed. She had become an author of teenage fiction and was interviewed about her most recent book.

Simon was a retired professor and lived with his wife, Lila, in a senior community. Lila was very active; he was not. He liked to read and have lunch once a month with some former colleagues. Simon thought it would be good to e-mail Joann. So he did, and found out what had happened in the forty-five years since they had seen each other. They started to keep contact with each other by e-mail, and when they could, they "Skyped" each other on their computer cameras. For Simon it was not the same as seeing her in person, however, so they planned a meeting. They spotted each other immediately and kissed as if all those years hadn't flown by. Joann seemed to Simon to be just as vivacious and sweet as she was when they were dating each other in high school. She was as pretty as ever, and Simon felt just as he did back then. They began seeing each other and he knew he was very much in love with her.

After high school, Simon had gone off to college in New York and Joann went to college in Baltimore. Their young romance couldn't overcome the distance and time, but now they felt as if they had never been apart. Simon was married and had two children and a grandchild; Joann was a widow with three children. They were in love and they wanted to live happily ever after. Simon and Lila did little to have fun together, and after Simon met Joann in that restaurant in Baltimore, he had an affair with her and decided to leave his marriage.

Simon came to therapy with Lila, but he was determined to leave, even after long talks about the time and love they had invested in each other, their children, and grandchildren. There was no compromising with Simon. He didn't want to evaluate his situation in six months or try a trial separation. His irrational thinking was challenged, but he was determined.

SIMON: *I did all that was expected of me, but now as I get nearer to the end, I am going to make the choice to be with Joann. I am not proud of that decision, but I am going to do it.*

Lila stayed in therapy to try to understand and to help her cope with her pain and find a way for her to live this new life.

Homosexual Affairs

When a married man believes he is homosexual, he is confronted with many issues. He must first tell his wife. He knows this will be very difficult, whether she suspects he is homosexual or is completely in the dark. Either way, it will be shocking information. Her entire life comes crashing down around her and, unlike the reaction to other infidelities, she feels sure her marriage is over. She is concerned about sexually transmitted diseases (STDs); what and when to tell the children; and above all, how she could have missed it. He has some of the same concerns. For many, the most difficult part is telling his parents and his siblings and, hardest of all, his children. He may need to explain this to his friends. His life will change drastically.

Their marriage was formed on a completely different expectation, of course: a heterosexual relationship.

How to Deal with a Homosexual Affair

In these situations, the marriage most likely will end, although not all marriages do. A few try to keep the family under one roof and the man has a small apartment that he visits or lives in part-time. Some wait to end the marriage at a certain date, such as when the youngest child starts college. Some of these men even find that they aren't really homosexual or are bisexual, and they go back to their wife. While for most men, the realization that they are gay is an emotional relief, such a discovery is also unsettling because of the sudden changes he must make. The changes are very difficult for his wife, children, and parents as well. People find different solutions and different timetables depending on their specific situations. The ages of the children are of concern regarding what and when they are told. Foremost, you will have many questions, and you have every right to ask them. You also have every right to request STD testing.

It is very important to remember that if you have children, *your partner is still their father* and should be treated with compassion and respect. It is in the best interests of your children that they remember he is their father. You must handle the situation carefully and not with anger toward him where the children are concerned. In the best-case scenario, he will support them emotionally throughout their entire lives, and financially until they are eighteen. The children will expect him to celebrate their birthdays in some way, and to be there for holidays and for their graduations and weddings. One day, he may be a grandfather and should be involved in his grandchildren's lives. If this is what he wants, you should help to make it happen. *Not* allowing it to happen will burden all of your children's lives.

Clearly, you will have a tough time as well. You will be grieving the loss of the life that you expected and wanted. Holidays and birthdays will be painful, but the pain will dissipate over the years. You will question why you didn't recognize the situation, and review your life together again and again. This is part of the process of making shocking news part of a person's history. If you do remarry, try to find it in your heart to let your ex-husband be part of the family. Others have made this happen in their family; it is not impossible.

Though it is difficult, families can recover from a homosexual affair if they can learn to handle their anger. This is important, and seeking professional help is advisable. It is something that you do for your family so that you can allow them to have a father, regardless of your feelings. And you do this so that you do not become embittered.

Remember: He did not do this to harm or hurt anyone. He didn't choose it; it happened.

Also remember that if the marriage ends, you will be building a new life for yourself and your children, if you have any. I suggest you find *new traditions*; establish a new way to celebrate. Do the holidays differently. Celebrate with friends. Take a family vacation instead of observing the holidays in the usual way. Feed the homeless on Thanksgiving, then go out for dinner. Be creative and think of things that are different yet still bring you together.

Exercise

1. Did you see your husband's affair in this chapter? Yes/No
   If "Yes," what was it?
2. In every reason for an affair in this chapter, a fundamental problem was effective communication. Is this a problem that you and your husband experience? Yes/No
3. Do one of the following indicate how you feel?
   Powerless: Yes/No
   Angry: Yes/No
   Hurt: Yes/No
   Powerful: Yes/No
   Write down any other feelings that describe you:

   _____

4. Did any of the affairs discussed in this chapter describe your experience? Yes/No
5. What thoughts do you have for self-help?

chapter eight

MEN, POWER, AND CONTROL

Farther up the continuum of affairs we come to those that can be more difficult to resolve. These affairs are related to power and control. Some of these men are very boastful as a way of proving they are real men, and others are truly very successful and accomplished. What they have in common is that they attract women, but treat them poorly. Many of these men are the powerful ones we read about in news stories; yet in the realm of interpersonal relations they may not be so accomplished. How do we explain this? Why do they risk everything?

The men at this point in the continuum have affairs to feel good about themselves and to fill the emptiness from within with excitement. For some, having an affair is the way to avoid emotional intimacy with their spouse, for as the couple in a relationship becomes closer and the intimacy increases, this type of husband's anxiety rises. He handles this by distancing himself from her, arguing, or by forming a triangle. One way to form a triangle is by having sex with someone else. Other ways to create a triangle are to become overinvolved in some activity so that the intimacy is replaced by investing time and energy in something else, like work, a sport, or alcohol. A triangle with another woman can keep him from having too much intimacy with either woman, and then sex will temporarily give him relief from the anxiety for a while. These affairs are usually *serial affairs* or *flings*. Of course, if he starts to feel intimacy developing in his affair, his anxiety will rise. He then will end the affair and look for another.

Macho Men

You recognize the "macho man" right away because he is the one who needs to give everyone, including himself, the message that he is a *man*. One of the most important ways he does that is to have sex with as many women as he can, and to tell his friends in advance of his plan, then brag about it to them, and delight in their approval. This is different from the sexually addicted man, who is coping with anxiety that can only be reduced through sex, and at that just temporarily. He starts thinking about sex until his thoughts cause him to become more tense. When his anxiety increases, he looks for sex, has sex, and starts the cycle all over again with his thinking. The macho man finds sex whenever the opportunity presents itself, but the addict is always searching. The macho man is doing it to make himself feel more like a man, but the addict is doing it purely to sustain the high from his sexual addiction. (See Chapter 9 for a more thorough discussion of sexual addiction.)

Psychiatrist Frank Pittman refers to macho men as "philanderers." He writes, in *Man Enough*:

> Philanderers require a steady change of sexual partners to protect themselves from making and keeping a commitment to just one person. . . . The gender attitudes and philandering pattern may come from the culture or may come from the family, and are passed on from father to son, generation after generation. Masculinity can be achieved in two ways—by competing with other men or by exerting dominance over women. . . . Philanderers may be hostile and cruel to women, using seduction to humiliate them, or they may be intimidated and frightened by women to such a degree that they use seduction to tame them.

Macho men come in many disguises. For example, they can be like Stanley Kowalski, as most famously played by Marlon Brando, in *A Streetcar Named Desire*, or like Ray Charles, played by Jamie Foxx in the movie *Ray*. Basically, the macho man does not really care for women: He is angry at them. He likes to be with other men; they are his cheering section. His friends admire and support his behavior, make jokes, and also get a kick out of devaluing women. They are giving him positive feedback about his behavior. It may be that his father, uncles, or grandfathers treated women this way—even though these women might have been his mother and aunts or grandmothers. His friends cover for the affair, or do whatever they can to help him fool his wife. These are men who have not grown up emotionally and have not seriously taken on their responsibility as husbands or fathers. Having sex makes them feel manly, and reporting how great it was to their admiring friends makes the macho man feel even manlier.

How to Deal with a Macho Man's Affair

If you are married to a macho man, you must speak with him about the behavior you have observed.

1. Rehearse what you want to say before starting your conversation. This helps to reduce the anger and frustration when you actually speak with him.
2. Pick a quiet time to be alone, to have uninterrupted privacy.
3. Without anger, tell him you have serious concerns. Example: "Bob, you are going out alone with the boys. I have reason to suspect there may be other women involved. I am unhappy and concerned about this behavior and the future of our marriage. I have made an appointment with a marriage therapist to help us make changes. The appointment is at (time, date)."

He may answer in the negative, or discount what you are saying. Make your appointment anyway. If he shows up, that is a good sign. If he doesn't, you must keep the appointment yourself, and work with someone who can guide you through the rough times. At the end, you will know more about what you can do than you do now.

Jonathan and Maggie

Jonathan and Maggie came in for counseling because she felt he ignored her and spent too much time "with the boys." Jonathan looked like the poster boy for the all-American young man. He managed a tennis club and played a lot of tennis himself. Maggie taught kindergarten and looked just like the teacher all children dream of having—sweet, smiling, and pretty.

MAGGIE: *We've been married a year and the excitement has worn off. It's as though I'm not there.*
JONATHAN: *Well, nobody can keep up with that kind of excitement. We have sort of settled down. Tennis is an invigorating game. I play, I teach, and I run the program. My responsibilities have increased since I've become manager.*

This sounded like the typical response of a couple who is at a point where passion begins to decline, but as Maggie went on, it was clear that something else was happening.

MAGGIE: *But when we go to a bar, you dump me and laugh it up and drink for hours with your friends. I am sitting alone. You are not there with me.*

As Maggie was speaking, Jonathan "zoned out" and was not listening.

When I spoke to him about it, he claimed to not know what I meant. But it was clear that either Maggie's worries did not concern him enough to listen, or his anxiety was rising and he was removing himself from the present, from his wife's concern.

We discussed scheduling, so they would make time for each other and time for evenings out. Before the week was out, Maggie called to say that she had a phone call from a friend who saw Jonathan out for dinner and acting romantically toward another woman when he was supposed to be at a business meeting.

At first, Jonathan denied this. Then Maggie said she was going to hire a private investigator, and showed him the brochures she had collected from three of them. Jonathan acquiesced and told her it was true, but the woman meant nothing to him.

That part was true: The woman meant nothing to him, but it was becoming more and more apparent that neither did his wife and that Jonathan had a serious problem.

Maggie didn't believe what Jonathan had said about the other woman. Because her father had cheated on her mother, "I know the type and what to do," she told me. "So I hired a PI to see if Jonathan was behaving like my dad and if I was on the right track."

Although Jonathan came to therapy, he was reluctant to work on their problems. A few weeks later, Maggie had evidence that Jonathan had continued the affair, and also had another one going on. Now she knew he was having serial affairs.

Jonathan's Behavior

Jonathan is a good example of the macho man who is basically more interested in having sex with multiple partners than he is with developing a faithful and loving relationship with his wife. He has a closer relationship with his male friends than he does with his wife. When Jonathan was confronted with this fact, he finally started to cooperate. We discussed his family history, which showed two generations of men having affairs. His father had a series of affairs, and had separated from his mother a number of times. Jonathan grew up as the youngest of four brothers, all of whom have had affairs. What was it that caused this to start? Jonathan knew that his grandfather had what Jonathan's family called "a roaming eye." This phrase showed that in his family not only was infidelity not taken seriously, it was the way the men were taught to behave. In talking with Jonathan, he admitted it was "a male thing" and had nothing to do with Maggie.

There was much work to be done. Maggie thought she was not being taken seriously, was betrayed by Jonathan without remorse, and that he, like his family, minimized the audacity of this behavior. She was right, because Jonathan had grown up in a family where no thought was given to a woman's feelings. Women were just disregarded. The women he had affairs with were treated similarly. He made no emotional connection with the women because he was incapable of making a connection. For this reason, his affairs were serial affairs.

This case is difficult to work with, but much can be accomplished if the man is as committed as the wife to working it out. Jonathan said he was.

JONATHAN: *When I look at myself, I am not proud. In fact, I feel empty inside and I try to fill it by being with people. That makes me forget it for a little while, but it comes back.*

Conclusion

Jonathan was referred to a therapist for individual therapy to work on his feeling of "emptiness."

Maggie continued having sessions with me to understand why she had been so attracted to a man like Jonathan. They said they were committed to working on the marriage. She and Jonathan continued to see me to work on recovery from the infidelity. They both had a lot of work to be done, but what was the alternative? That would be for Jonathan to continue feeling empty and having affairs and for Maggie to not understand her choice in a mate. With this help they could grow together and have a meaningful life.

Men with Power

Women are attracted to powerful men. The characteristics that make men powerful are appealing to women. When a man excels at what he does, whether he is an actor, doctor, singer, ball player, lawyer, or politician, this draws admiration, especially if it is combined with leadership qualities and charisma. He doesn't need to have the looks of a movie star, but he has to be important and have power in what he does. Former Secretary of State Henry Kissinger, who was accompanied about Washington by many beautiful and famous women, certainly fits this description. When asked about this phenomenon, he replied that "Power is the great aphrodisiac."

The powerful man can be found almost everywhere. He has a formidable position—head of his office, whether it is law, medical, real estate, engineering, a hospital, a laboratory, or a television program. He can be a college professor, lawyer, doctor, rabbi, minister, prince, senator, or president. Many women like the man who is respected by everybody. Some feel excitement from his leadership, most feel protected, and some feel a rise in self-esteem for having gained his attention. Others find he fills their needs because of his qualities, and some can project other qualities onto him that fulfill their emotional needs.

We often hear of this scenario in academia, where the boundaries have loosened between professor and student, and also in politics and Hollywood. The bottom line is that women are attracted to men with power.

Power on Display

Power is found in every corridor of government buildings in our nation's capital. Every position has a name—the shorter the title, the more power. The President has more power than the Vice-President, who has more than the Secretary of Commerce, and he more than the Assistant Secretary of Commerce; and so it goes. Everyone is aware of status and power. In Washington, power is also measured in access. How close is your office to the Deputy Assistant or the Assistant Deputy Assistant? There was a time when the many romantic affairs in Washington were ignored by the press, so the public was not aware of them. Of course, that's not the case anymore!

Powerful men having affairs continue to make headlines. One of the most shocking was Tiger Woods, a much-admired American sports hero and clean-cut individual. At the same time he is an enigma because of his serial affairs. Senator John Edwards also presented himself as an American hero for his populous beliefs, but he lost the faith of the American public, and with it the presidential nomination of the Democratic Party, when he had a year-long affair while his wife Elizabeth was fighting metastasized cancer. In 2010, he acknowledged that he was the father of a little girl and he and Elizabeth were divorcing.

They were men with power, and they have a protective staff who make things happen for them and what they did offends the values of most Americans. Because we read of these people, we can see the effect of their use and abuse of power. But this happens to other people in other places, although it does not make it into the news media.

NOT ALL POWERFUL MEN CHEAT

Even though some men with power have all the ingredients necessary for an affair, not all men in leadership respond to women who show interest or initiate an inappropriate relationship or an affair. Such men do not need the adulation of women or having affairs with them to sustain their belief in themselves or to solve emotional issues they have. They are there to do their work and have a solid sense of self and a purpose in their jobs.

Power at the Local Level

Some of the same power issues go on at the local level, but are not usually reported in the newspapers. Nevertheless, hearts are broken by some of the powerful and controlling men. Many women married to a man who is in a public position because he is a rabbi or minister or doctor are aware that other women may be attracted to him, and that he could have an affair. If he does, it is not long before everyone knows that he is having an affair or is "sleeping around."

How to Deal with a Powerful Man's Affair

If your partner fits the description of a man with power, and you suspect he is having an affair, you need an answer and a solution because dealing with his affair can be a very public experience. To minimize the damage to your family, keep a low profile, avoid public statements, and choose carefully those women you share your problems with—only true friends.

Whether or not you two are still together, it's vital that you first attend to your emotions, so find a mental health professional to help you with this. When your emotions have calmed down, you then can begin the process of creating a new life that is completely separate from the life you had—one that was based on his power. One way to begin is to join a support group—you may well find other women like you who are facing the same challenges. Make new friends, find work of your own if you hadn't worked before and would like to, or explore any interest or hobby that you have never given the time to. Now is the time to build confidence that you are your own worthy individual if that has been an issue for you.

Jessica and Mathew

Let's look at Jessica, who came to my office. She was quiet, but soon lost her composure as she spoke of the way her life has changed. She and her husband divorced, and she had to start many parts of her life over in a way that was different from that of many other women. This was due to her husband's prominent position as a minister.

I first met Jessica in a woman's support group. She was very thin, drawn-looking, and tearful. She started telling the other women her story.

JESSICA: *I've had to move out of the parish. Everything I did was associated with the church. I no longer have a home. Having always lived in parish homes, we have no equity. I live now in a one-room studio apartment—the best I could afford. I also lost belonging to my church. I feel that the ministers at other churches know me and know my husband, Mathew. I have lost most of my friends and my job. My job was with the church as his wife. I ran many of the programs, had teas, and did the many things expected of the minister's wife. So I feel as though I am starting over at this age. He married her last week and today I am falling apart over it.*

Jessica received empathy from the women and they offered her suggestions from their experience. In a private counseling session, Jessica said that she did not want her former husband to come in with her to talk, but she had many bottled-up emotions to rid herself of. She had been treated poorly by a man she had expected better from, and she was very disappointed in him. Jessica needed the opportunity to talk and to express her pain and anger and especially her bitterness over the unfairness of her situation. That helped, but Jessica also needed help connecting with a community of women and planning the next stage of her life. We worked together to increase her assets, which meant finding a career, joining a support group, and teaching her how to fill her empty hours with some meaningful activities.

Other wives of powerful and well-known men in their communities tell similar stories. Besides being embarrassed by the husband's betrayal, many women lose their jobs because they had helped manage the husband's business, or dental or medical practice, or restaurant. The women feel as though they have lost control of their lives. It is important to regain control over their lives. Many of the women in Jessica's support group became a community for her by helping her to celebrate holidays like Thanksgiving and Christmas. Most women who were married to well-known husbands are wealthy and do not have concerns over money, but some (like Jessica) do.

Men Who Need to Control

Although many powerful men are kind and treat people fairly, some men find the need to *control*—their work, their spouse, their children, and so on. This type of man will *also* control the other woman and how the affair proceeds. People admire these men because they are helpful and are the center of a busy and important organization, whether it is their medical office or the Oval Office. They receive acclamation, admiration and, sometimes, flirtations from those who work for them. Most such men do not return that attention, but many do, especially the men who love to live with excitement and danger, and enjoy being the center of attention. Men in this category are usually charming. They have an outer bravura and many are very successful, but they have their own personal issues and look to affairs to cover up their emptiness.

THE RISKS OF MARRYING A POWERFUL MAN

Marrying a successful, powerful man should not be a risk for infidelity, but unfortunately it is, because of all the women who are attracted to him and the emotional needs that he may have. In addition, because the men in the halls of power are so visible, the public can see what is happening if a marriage unravels.

Dealing with a Controlling Man's Affair

If you have a controlling husband, you most likely are afraid of him. Often, this kind of man seemed decisive in the beginning of the marriage and you admired that; now, however, it seems that you are in a prison, unable to assert yourself and with no rights. What seemed like someone to watch over you now feels like a prison guard. If this seems familiar to you, you must understand and believe that you do have rights. You can speak, voice your opinions, and do things you want as long as they do no harm. The way you do this is through communication. It does not have to be aggressive, but assertive. If you become aggressive, you will be like him, loud and demanding. In Chapter 11, you'll learn how to use the "I" message, which is a tool that allows you to make statements about what you want to do and to be assertive. You must, however, be certain that your husband does not get threatening, and is not physically or verbally abusive. If he is, see a therapist to help you and your husband learn to speak with each other. You cannot put yourself in a dangerous situation.

In most cases with difficult husbands, the first step is to use your communication skills. If this does not seem to change the unwanted behavior—the abuse of power, control, and not recognizing your rights—going to a therapist is the next step. A therapist can get to the underlying reasons for this behavior, which may be his childhood or family experience.

Bev and Josh

Josh was a *controller* when he married Bev. She was very kind and very pretty, but most of all for Josh, she could be controlled. She seemed bewildered by the world and he felt he could guide her. It made him feel protective. As the years went by, however, she became angry because she felt she was always in a power struggle with him. Josh came for counseling reluctantly: It was not the kind of thing he would do. Bev found out that he was having an affair with their neighbor, Geri, and she threatened to tell Geri's husband if Josh didn't come for counseling.

Josh and Bev came into my office on a crisp day in October. I remember this because he admitted to the affair after minimizing it and then promised to give it up after Thanksgiving—two months away. He did what controllers do, and tried to take over the therapy by telling me what he would agree to do. He had decided that this was fair to both women because his wife would have Christmas with him. After I told him that this was not acceptable, he told me if he didn't wait until after Thanksgiving, Geri's brothers would probably slash Bev's tires. Of course, he was using threats and grasping at straws. He was being forced to give up control and end this affair. It was hard for him to do, because he needed order in his life and he wanted to control everything that pertained to it. He was also surprised when Bev said that she felt like a prisoner in their marriage.

Conclusion

Part of our work together was to review family history, because that gives insight to family behavior, values, and messages. Josh had lived through a very unhappy childhood with a controlling and sadistic father. Josh was surprised at the understanding and empathy he received from us because this had not been his experience in his family-of-origin.

Josh had work to do because he didn't feel comfortable when he had to give up control. One of the reasons a person keeps control is because he doesn't trust others; he feels he can rely only on himself. To keep that control, he must know where everything is, that all systems are in place in case anything goes wrong. Bev's finding out about his affair threw everything into chaos from his viewpoint, and he struggled to get control. When Josh lost control, it was as if he had lost all his bearings. Josh needed control because that gave him power; when he lost control, he panicked because he was once again that little boy who had no power, just a feeling of emptiness.

Exercise

1. Have you read anything in this chapter that applies to your husband's affair? Yes/No
     If "Yes," what is it?
2. Do you and your husband have the closeness and ability to share your feelings and fears with each other comfortably?
3. Do you tell him your concerns? Yes/No
4. Does he share his concerns with you? Yes/No
5. Are you finding time each day to talk? Yes/No
6. Do you find time each week for a family meeting? Yes/No
7. Did anything you read in this chapter apply to you, in terms of your feelings and reactions to your husband? Yes/No
8. If "Yes," what was it?
9. What can you do about it?

chapter nine

MEN WITH PERSONALITY ISSUES

Along the continuum of reasons why men cheat, we now reach the endpoint, where men have affairs because of *personality issues*. I call these individuals *poor-risk partners* because the risk is poor that they will be faithful. They are men who usually have serial affairs. In general, they are incapable of making an emotional connection to their wife or to any of the many women with whom they have affairs.

These individuals have *personality traits* that make them difficult to get along with and cause problems in maintaining other relationships as well, not just romantic relationships. They have a long history of stormy relationships starting in their teenage years and continuing throughout their lifespan.

The men in these categories can be exasperating to live with. They all have emotional problems that overwhelm them, and many have affairs to help cope. These problems not only disturb their marital relationships, but many other aspects of their day-to-day life. Unfortunately, most such men don't believe this to be true and do not come for therapy. Yet, they need to have a therapist to treat them, to offer support, and to help them understand themselves.

If you are married to such a man, you can become so involved in trying to meet an endless series of unreasonable expectations and needs and trying to cope with repeated disappointments that life loses its joy, leaving you feeling discouraged or depressed. It is important to take care of yourself and to find a therapist, a support group for yourself, and other ways to nurture yourself. Although it is difficult, it is also important to find help for your husband and encourage him to enter treatment so that hopefully he can stop his affairs and begin to learn how to be empathic, which is very important to a relationship.

In this chapter, we will discuss people with narcissistic traits; other groups who are frequently argumentative and difficult to get along with; and those with sexual addictions. There are still other personality disorders that make a man a poor risk, but these are the most common.

The Narcissist

The term "narcissistic" is derived from the word *narcissus,* and comes from a Greek myth in which a young man named Narcissus saw his reflection in a pond. He could not stop gazing at himself and soon fell in love with his own image. Nymphs and girls fell in love with him, but he was not tempted by them. One who fell in love with Narcissus was Echo, but Narcissus only had eyes for himself. Echo was so in despair by the unrequited love that she faded away and all that became of her was a whisper. Narcissus was so captivated by his own reflection that he fell into the water and drowned. The nymphs also grieved for Narcissus, and in the place where he bent over the pool to gaze at his face a beautiful flower grew. It is called a narcissus.

TWO PEOPLE, ONE LOVE?

As one woman told me, "The trouble with being married to a narcissistic man is that you are both in love with the same person."

Narcissistic Characteristics

Like Narcissus, people who are *narcissistic,* or have similar traits, see themselves as perfect, so they believe that if there is a problem, it must lie somewhere other than with themselves. Following are other characteristics typical of narcissists.

Attractive and Charming

Narcissistic individuals can initially seem very attractive because they are usually charming, dress well, seem to be very pleasant and socially adept, and are highly self-confident. Because those with narcissistic traits lack concern for others, they do not hesitate to make demands without taking into consideration others' feelings or circumstances or whether what they are asking is inconvenient.

Sense of Entitlement

Narcissistic individuals also have an extreme sense of entitlement and think only in terms of how events affect them. They put themselves first. In fact, they hardly notice anyone else, except if they need them in some way to promote their own concerns. For example, if a narcissistic person received a phone call from a friend who was going to pick him up to go to the ball game but who had just had a serious car accident, the narcissistic person would probably respond by saying something like, "Does that mean we're not going to the ball game?" Then he would be preoccupied with how to get his ticket and how to get to the game anyway, and would never think of asking how his friend was.

Lack of Empathy

Narcissists have little or no empathy for others. They seldom come to therapy because they do not feel they have problems. In fact, they have a very high regard for themselves. In her aptly titled book *Why Is It Always About You?* social worker Sandy Hotchkiss writes, "The hallmark of mature love is reciprocity, in which two people have as much regard for each other as they do for themselves. The narcissist, in contrast, does not love in any mature, reciprocal, or nurturing sense of the word."

Here are some of the remarks made by women who have been married to narcissists:

CAROLYN: *When I went into labor, Jack dropped me off at the hospital because he had tickets for a tennis match.*
JACK: *I wasn't going to cancel because there is nothing I could do. I don't know how to deliver babies.*

Note: There was no empathy for what his wife would be going through, nor her fear or apprehension, not to mention concern or curiosity about their new baby.

JANET: *When our daughter was singing a solo at church, he wouldn't go even for her part, because he wanted to read the Sunday papers.*

Note: There was no concern for his daughter's feelings, no interest in how she would do, and no thought of being there to support her.

LAURA: *When my car broke down late at night on the freeway and I had to wait half an hour for the tow truck, I called Lloyd. He wouldn't come to stay with me or wait for the tow truck, even though I was stuck five minutes from home. I was very frightened.*

Note: Her husband showed no concern for her safety or her fear.

JOY: *When Robert and I decided to redesign our kitchen, Robert had it done while I was on a two-week visit to my mother 3,000 miles away. On my return, I cried and would not speak to Robert for weeks.*

Note: Robert was shocked. Like all narcissists, he couldn't understand someone else's feelings. He thought Joy would be happy and did not notice how much she wanted to redesign the kitchen herself. She was not consulted on any choices and she hated the Early American kitchen he chose because she had been hoping for a contemporary one (which she had discussed with Robert). Now she wonders if he was even listening.

Underindulged Childhoods
Some narcissists grow up in a home where the children are ignored and not given praise or encouragement. If a young child is brought up in a cold home by individuals who show no warmth or appreciation, the child does not develop inner confidence, good self-esteem, and personal pride in himself. Therefore, he must search for it from others. Most important, he never learned empathy for others. He becomes completely self-absorbed searching for approval, but is unlikely to give it to others.

Overindulged Childhoods
The other side of the coin is the overindulged child, who gets everything he wants. He comes to expect that all his wants will be addressed, even at great effort, by his parents.

This concept is carried out as an adult. He has developed a strong sense of entitlement. He does not think of others, only of his needs, which he believes should be met.

Incapable of Loyalty
Narcissistic men do not usually stay faithful, because they need the constant adulation that comes from a new love. The thrill of adulation then wears off very quickly. Not even passion can sustain the high

levels of attention and appreciation needed by the narcissist. He can also, just like the macho man, be known as a womanizer because he gets what he wants and then retreats, discarding the woman and going on to the next one.

Dealing with a Narcissist

If you are married to a narcissist, you may begin to lose a sense of identity because your feelings, actions, and very existence are continually invalidated or ignored by him. If he has an affair, your situation seems even more desperate. It is important to rebuild your sense of identity and self-esteem. It's also time to surround yourself with people who recognize your talents and value to the world. Focus on what you're good at or always wanted to do. Remind yourself that what you feel is real and that you deserve love and attention. Try to understand that his personality developed long before he met you. These problems are not a reflection of you.

In addition, therapy—both for you and your family—can be very helpful. You will learn to set limits for your narcissist's behavior. Children often believe something is wrong with them when their highly successful father doesn't care about them. These children probably have not received the interest, praise, and encouragement from their father that they need to thrive. It may even become a competition for praise between father and child. The atmosphere in the home of a narcissist revolves around him, and no one else.

One wife told me that her husband's team was receiving recognition for their legal work at a company dinner. His teenage daughter was angry and refused to attend, cried, and threatened to run away from home if her parents went. There was no compromise. The father looked upon it as a bluff, so the parents went to the ceremony. When they came home, they found that their daughter was still at home. This is the story of the turmoil in a narcissist's family.

Ellen and Kyle

Ellen came into my office heartbroken because her husband, Kyle, was going to leave her for someone named Rosa, who worked for him. As her story unfolded, it became clear that Kyle cared very little for Ellen's feelings. Kyle refused to join Ellen initially in our sessions. Ellen had made her first appointment in July, even though she had found out about the affair a few months earlier.

ELLEN: *I suspected he was having an affair last May when he went off a few times by himself, once during our anniversary weekend. I called the resort we always stayed at when we were in Mazatlan and asked to speak to Mr. and Mrs. Albert and was told that I would be connected, but I quickly hung up before the connection was made. I confronted him and he denied it and said his many weekends away were work-related. It was possible because I have known for a while that his work was the most important aspect of his life, but this was our wedding anniversary and we always celebrated by going to Mazatlan in Mexico over Memorial Day weekend. We met there twenty years ago. It is . . . I guess I should say was . . . a romantic spot for us. I was furious. I didn't know what to be angrier about—the fact that it was our place and our anniversary date, or that he was cheating. I mean how could he? How could he? The part that was so infuriating was that he couldn't get it that this was sacred to us, and he desecrated it. I know the picture is bigger than that, but I can't get over it.*

In our further discussions, it seemed that Kyle did not understand the depth of Ellen's feelings and that many times he did not meet her needs in situations that would have been obvious to others, like having an affair at a place that she thinks of as sacred to them. Ellen is an only child and had been close to her parents. Ten years earlier, when her parents died in an automobile accident, Kyle did not accompany her to their funeral—his work always came first. There were other times, happier ones, but he was not there to celebrate many of their children's events, including graduations, recitals, and sports events. Most were missed because of work for the company he built and headed, or because he considered the children's sports events and recitals to be minor.

Throughout their marriage, Kyle had shown little to no empathy for his wife or for their children. He had been self-absorbed. In the one session we had together, he complained that Ellen did not put his business first. Owning his own business had been a goal of his since he was a kid, and he let nothing stand in his way of achieving that. He said that Ellen just "didn't get it; and she often attended to others before me and my business needs." However, the reverse was true. Ellen often put his desires first. Her stories of their life together indicated that she collaborated with him many times to put the children's needs second to his, joining him rather than finding a compromise or attending to the children first.

ELLEN DESCRIBED KYLE'S CHILDHOOD AND HIS WORK:
Kyle was adored by his parents. They always told him he would do something great. Maybe he will. His accomplishments are impressive at this point in time. He works on individualizing medical treatment using a person's DNA and even predicting possible trouble spots for someone. These are notable accomplishments and goals. His parents are very proud of him. They "live and breathe" for him. So, you see, he didn't come from an abusive home or one where the parents criticized him. He was an only child and they adored him.

Ellen is right in saying his parents were not abusive, but they were guilty of overdoing their praise. Kyle grew up thinking he was so very special that he thinks only of himself. He has a sense of entitlement, which is the hallmark of narcissism, and is oblivious to how others feel. He just doesn't think of others, though he does think highly of himself. Intimacy is something narcissistic people cannot develop, *because they have no empathy and they cannot build a close relationship.* They are empty inside.

After about three months into my sessions with Ellen, Kyle came along with her for her appointment, but only for one session. He was very handsome and dressed stylishly. At first, he was all charm as he talked about his work, but that soon disappeared when we talked about Ellen's feelings. He showed no remorse for the pain Ellen felt from his infidelity and felt he was entitled to a new life with Rosa. I asked him what he thought was most important in his life.

KYLE: *Accomplishments. Everyone must work toward that.*

I asked, "What if there is a conflict with achieving that goal?"

KYLE: *I would not let anything stand in the way.*

There were many times when work won out, even when it conflicted with the very serious needs of his children. In addition, he described Rosa, who was from Argentina, as a very beautiful woman who worked actively with him on his executive team. In fact, he spoke glowingly of Rosa to Ellen without being aware of how it pained her. Ellen seemed to be used to this abusive behavior and did not speak up about it. When I pointed out to both of them that this was painful, Kyle announced that he had bought a condo for Rosa and himself and that Rosa was now decorating it. This was not a midlife crisis—this was a man completely incapable of understanding anyone else's feelings. Ellen was astonished.

A few days before Thanksgiving, Ellen called in tears.

ELLEN: *Kyle is leaving for good. He said he would send someone around to pick up his clothes. He refused my request to come talk with the children because he thought I was making too much of it. The children are heartbroken, not only that Thanksgiving and Christmas are completely ruined, but they understand their family life is changing terribly for everyone. Our eldest son is furious and swears he will never speak to his father again. Kyle has disappointed the children many times, but this was not just disappointment. This was real destruction.*

Conclusion

Kyle was incapable of understanding the enormous impact that leaving their mother for another woman would have on his children. In the best-case scenario, the parents sit down with the children and explain what is happening and how it will affect everyone's lives. They answer questions, give reassurances, and tell the children what they can expect, such as when the children will see their father, where and when he can be reached, and that the rules will change as they try together to make this separation work.

Ellen continued therapy to understand why the marriage failed; she still believed that she was to blame. Her children also started therapy.

The Unstable, Moody Person

Another person in the poor-risk partner category is one whose behavior and emotions are unstable and frequently and dramatically change. While we are all prone to changes in our mood, this person's moodiness is extreme. One minute he can be happy; then he will get very angry over something minor; then he may become explosive. He can love you one day and become enraged at you the next. People notice that they get angry a lot when they are with him. He has had difficulty in maintaining relationships since he was young.

Such people seem to get into arguments more than most and may have difficulty in school and in holding jobs. These individuals may attempt to regulate their emotional problems through the use of alcohol and drugs. They may also engage in risky behaviors, such as reckless driving or gambling. They can be very standoffish, but may also become very clingy. Basically, this person is afraid of abandonment. His problems came from his home life as a child, where he did not develop a secure sense of attachment to his parents. He is, therefore, uneasy about issues of abandonment, questions people's behavior, and often misinterprets what someone means. At times he can be unpleasant, and at times very nice, but in general he is very hard to live with because of his misreading situations. When he says something belittling, he is responding with anger, not with understanding. When he suspects his ultimate fear, he becomes clingy and very frightened, or his fear leads him to be argumentative. When the relationship becomes too close, his anxiety rises because he cannot tolerate too much closeness just as he fears abandonment. He is moody because he doesn't trust, and his outbursts of anger come from that.

Psychiatrist Irwin Marcus describes the men in this category: "In their affairs, and in their marriage, this personality may manifest itself as mentally or physically cruel in association with taking sadistic pleasure in humiliating women. . . . His tendency to be too demanding without giving much back leads to divorce in many situations."

Dealing with a Moody, Unstable Partner

The best way to deal with this kind of person is to put a stop to his behavior. That means setting limits as one would do with a child by using the "I" message. You will learn more about this in Chapter 11, but the basic form is: **I will _____ if you continue _____.** *Then you must do it.* It becomes a *consequence* for the behavior rather than a *punishment*.

Living with such a person means that you must set limits at times when he doesn't respect the boundaries for relationships. In essence, you are giving him controls he doesn't at that moment possess.

You can verbally set boundaries by saying things like, "I won't go for a walk with you if you don't stop shouting." "I will not go to the dinner party with you until your mood changes." "I will leave the room if you continue banging on the table." "Watch TV for an hour, and then if you are not so angry, we will go. If you are still angry, I will go alone."

If you notice, the consequences may seem subtle, but they are his biggest fears—not being included, being abandoned, being left out. Yet they are not threats, because he has a choice.

Joan and Robert

Joan came into my office crying because Robert was having another affair. This time he was cheating on Joan because he cannot control his reactions to her upcoming visits to her mother, which he experiences as a personal abandonment. He feels alone and frightened, and his reaction is to find another person to cling to so that he will not feel abandoned.

JOAN: *Maybe I should just get used to it. This one started because I said I was going to visit my mother for a week and that set him off. He wants me to stay here and he finds a million excuses why I can't go. My sisters and I all live about a three-hour drive from her house, so we really have to stay over when we visit. He is unreasonable and says I probably have a boyfriend on the side. He says that to me*

when he is the one who has had many affairs! I know that to be true.
I don't know why he cheats on me.

Conclusion

In our work on this problem, I invited both Joan and Robert to my office. We went over carefully with Joan all she could do for Robert to ease his life while she was gone, even though that was not really the basic concern. It turns out that none of his concerns was legitimate—she had thought of everything.

> JOAN: *I found someone to walk the dog. All the meals are in the freezer, cooked and labeled. My mother is not in such good health and my sisters and I have divided up a schedule of visiting and taking her for her doctor's treatments. She is starting radiation treatments, every day for six weeks.*

Then we went over the ways that Joan could keep in touch and how often and when. In fact, when I asked about using a computer camera, Robert got very excited and wanted to buy one on their way home. His excitement comes from feeling less abandoned. I suggested that Joan stock up on DVDs for Robert to watch and to call him in the evenings to help him pick what to watch.

Robert made extra appointments with me during her absence and Joan was insightful enough to ignore the last affair after understanding the source of his problems. No progress was made with the cause of Robert's behavior because his personality type prevents him from understanding his feelings, and he would only become angry. The sessions merely dealt with actions that would reduce his anxiety and help him try to look at the reality of the situations that cause such anger. Joan did not leave Robert, because she had a family life, children, and an established lifestyle. She was in treatment to see if their problems could be worked out. Like all people with his issues, Robert could also have his charming moments; he wanted to run right out and buy her a computer camera and set it up so that they could use it. Joan wanted to see if she and Robert could work out this situation, which she considered an emergency. Upon her return, the serious work on their relationship began.

Needs of Narcissists and Moody People
Both types, the narcissistic individual and the clingy, moody one, become stressed when they believe they are losing what they need.

- The person with *narcissistic* traits needs someone to mirror back that he is as wonderful as he needs to believe he is, and he also needs someone who will support his sense of entitlement.
- People with an *unstable, moody personality* need someone who can put up with constantly and dramatically changing moods, unreasonable anger, and fears of abandonment.

These two types of people are often poor-risk partners not just because they are very difficult to live with due to their exhausting neediness, but because they have affairs as a way to help them cope. One needs to be told he is wonderful; the other that he is not being abandoned.

Sexual Addiction
Another member of the poor-risk partner group is the *sexually addicted* person. His life revolves around his compulsive need for sexual release. A person who is sexually addicted finds himself in a cycle that starts with him thinking about sex, and then he starts to compulsively pursue it. He may go to massage parlors or to prostitutes. Or he may fulfill his need for sexual excitement through the Internet, looking at pornographic websites or interacting with others in sexually explicit chatrooms. People find it hard to understand how a person can be addicted to something that is not a *substance*, like alcohol or drugs; however, sex addicts are actually affected by changes in their neurochemistry as they think about sex, and this continues throughout the process. Robert Weiss, a national authority on sexual addiction, explained that sex addicts enter a trancelike state as they begin their process of reducing the anxiety that builds. Finally, the anxiety is released through sexual activities.

Weiss explains that the body's release of adrenaline, dopamine, endorphins, and serotonin provide the addict with his drug. He writes, "Like the substance addict on his way to score drugs or the gambler walking into the casino, sex addicts are high on their own neurochemistry long before actually having sex." When a sexual experience ends, they are likely to experience feelings of anxiety and cravings for the next sexual encounter, even if there are also feelings of embarrassment and a wish to change the addiction.

Men who are sexually addicted have serial affairs because of this ongoing need. The sexually addicted person spends significant time and energy related to his addiction, seeking out the "high" that compulsive sexual activity brings him. If not engaged in sexual behavior, he is thinking of how next to act out his needs. He cannot stop thinking about this until it is finally satisfied. He spends time looking at pornography, which is easily found in abundance online; seeking prostitutes; hanging out at bars looking for women; and having phone sex. The Internet is his best bet for finding a way of coping with his sexual compulsivity, and he may spend eleven hours or more a day engaged in sexual activities. A hallmark of an *addiction is a sense of a loss of control over the addictive behavior—the individual feels compelled to engage in the behavior over and over again.*

Dealing with a Sex Addict

Hearing that your partner is a sex addict can be very frightening, and it's challenging to deal with that news in addition to the devastation of his affair. It sounds too overwhelming, and it is serious, but can be handled by someone trained in this specialty. When someone is sexually addicted, the therapist will treat that affair as any other would be treated, but with certain special considerations concerning the addiction, such as controls to help him overcome his addiction. Other considerations are joining a sexual addiction group, placing his computer in a public area of the house, limiting his use of the computer, blocking sexual sites, and having him keep a log to provide accountability for his comings and goings. He should attend a sexual addiction group, so that he can then call sponsors when his craving appears. His lifestyle could also include exercise and meditation.

In addition to personal therapy for his addiction, the sexual addict needs therapy to help him with the many issues related to his infidelity—*couples therapy*, because the marriage has been negatively impacted; and *family therapy*, because all members need to heal from the pain in the family.

Georgia and Craig

Georgia and Craig came in for marriage therapy because Georgia felt that Craig spent a lot of time away from the house, and when he was at home, he was withdrawn and sat alone in the upstairs den. We talked about their expectations for marriage and what they felt was missing. Craig was not active in the discussion and didn't participate even when this was pointed out to him. They made an appointment for the following week, but Georgia called before the appointment because she found a telephone bill with $800 charged to "900" calls. It was the first time that Georgia had seen these bills.

> GEORGIA: *It feels weird, really weird, like he's strange and what he does is weird. He's having sex to words he reads on a computer. You tell me that's normal?*

The couple was wealthy and usually their accountant took care of these bills, but Georgia had come across it. So the story came out bit by bit, session after session, that Craig was a sex addict. Craig tried to explain:

> CRAIG: *It just sort of happened. It is so easy to pick up a phone or go online. I just can't stop thinking about sex. I don't have physical contact with anyone, but this is just as bad because I am so preoccupied with it; and at the same time, I am so ashamed. Sex is always on my mind, but I feel it is not out of control because I only deal with fantasies online or on the phone. I see prostitutes, but not actual people.*

Georgia cringed as she heard this.

GEORGIA: *I feel as though I am married to a sick man. Are our children safe?*

Georgia's concerns were valid because she was married to a man who had a progressive illness that must be treated.

Conclusion
Both were referred to an addiction expert, who worked with them together and Craig alone on the addiction. It was hard for Georgia to do, but finally she stopped condemning Craig and realized that he was a sexual addict because he was ill with anxiety, and sex calmed him. I continued meeting with Georgia to help her recover from the shock and give her support during his recovery. We reviewed their life and established many of the things that would help, such as a time to talk, family meetings, exercise, dates, and family fun (which you will learn about in the concluding chapters).

Other Poor-Risk Partners
Other men fit into this category of poor-risk partners as well: those who have had many affairs and problems all their lives in relationships and work; those who have few or no friends; and those who may have been diagnosed as being sociopathic, bipolar, schizophrenic, or as having a chronic and debilitating mental illness. Such a man may have severe highs and lows, be physically violent, or isolate himself from you and from any social interactions. If this describes your partner, you may find yourself afraid of him. If so, find a therapist who can help you understand your particular situation. You need help as a couple, and he needs help as an individual in coping with this issue.

Many people in this category have difficult problems to deal with. The first approach is often called First Order changes, where you deal with issues that are priority and can help cope with the current anxiety. Second Order changes come later in treatment, when he can look deeper into causes and feelings, but at the present what feels like abandonment, nonappreciation, and anxiety must be addressed. The women married to these men need to understand their personality type and find how to cope with his behaviors from his therapist. She should try to keep the home life peaceful for the sake of the children, but should also self-nurture, find friends and support, and develop and pursue her interests.

Exercise

1. Do you feel as though you are walking on eggshells when you are with your partner? Yes/No
2. Are you afraid to express your opinion freely? Yes/No
3. Do you feel your opinion will be ridiculed or invalidated? Yes/No
4. When he is angry, can he find a way to cope with his anger? Yes/No
5. Does he notice your moods? Yes/No
6. If you are sad, is he concerned about you? Yes/No
7. Can you trust him to "be there" when you need him? Yes/No
8. Does he have an even temperament? Yes/No
9. If something happens to you, would he be concerned about you and your reaction first? Yes/No
10. Are you worried he will pass on a sexually transmitted disease to you? Yes/No
11. Does he leave for periods of time and not tell you where he is going? Yes/No
12. Do you feel he is overly concerned about his appearance? Yes/No
13. Has he ever had a problem with the law because of his temper or sexual issues? Yes/No
14. Are you frightened of him when he is angry? Yes/No
15. In a crisis, does he think of himself first? Yes/No
16. Does he fly off the handle frequently? Yes/No
17. Does he frequently misinterpret your behavior or what you say? Yes/No
18. Does he flirt with other women? Yes/No

19. Do you think he is too self-involved? Yes/No
20. Does he comes from a family where the father, brother, uncles, and/or cousins have affairs? Yes/No
21. Does he need to have privacy for his phone calls? Yes/No
22. Does he have friends you have not met? Yes/No
23. Do the friends you have met have affairs? Yes/No
24. Does he hide his whereabouts from you? Yes/No
25. Does he lie to you? Yes/No
26. Does he joke about the affairs he has had? Yes/No

If you answered "Yes" to most of these questions, you may be married to a man with one of the issues covered in this chapter. Individual counseling as well as couples counseling will help you clarify this.

Part III

RESTRUCTURING THE MARRIAGE

*"Fundamentally, therefore, any man
can, even under such circumstances,
decide what shall become of him —
mentally and spiritually."*

MAN'S SEARCH FOR MEANING BY DR. VIKTOR
FRANKL

*"Who is powerful?
He who conquers his passion."*

PIRKE AVOT 4:1, THE WISDOM OF THE FATHERS

chapter ten

DEALING WITH THE AFTERMATH OF THE AFFAIR

Typically, your reaction to the discovery that your husband or partner is having an affair is devastating. It feels as though a tsunami has swept over you. When you look around, nothing seems the same. The landscape that you were familiar with is now very strange. You don't know what to make of it and most important, you don't know what to do. It seems there is nothing to hang on to and you feel very much alone. This chapter will help you feel less alone and give you something to hang on to by helping you with your healing.

Your Reaction

The first step is that you must deal with the emotions you are experiencing. Understanding your emotions will begin to calm you because you will know what to expect and know that you are not alone: Others have gone through the same turmoil and survived. You are shocked and bewildered. Something has happened that you do not understand. What you believed to be true now seems in doubt. You may have believed in the purity and innocence of your marriage and now that has changed. You feel you no longer know it. You will be grieving your losses—it feels like a death. But this does not necessarily mean that your marriage is dead—it is reeling from what has happened.

Handling the Initial Fallout

You have likely already seen the severe collateral damage from the fallout of his affair. One is that, when discovered, it causes unbearable pain to those individuals he cares for—most of all, you. If, before he became involved with another woman, he would have tried to picture himself discussing it with you, explaining it to your children, telling his and your parents, his siblings, and his boss or colleagues, he might have taken a few steps back and really considered the ramifications.

Of course he didn't do that, so when you find out about the affair, a storm descends that will take years to clear. After the initial shock of the discovery, you need comfort to heal from the wounds of the affair. The first typical reaction is to go to a friend, *which may or may not be a good idea. It is a good idea if you trust her and if she can keep what you tell her confidential. If she can't, she is not the friend for you at this point in time.* It would be best to seek a mental health therapist. Remember, this is not a little wound. One man told me that the pain after an exposed affair produces more anguish than the problems in the marriage ever did. It takes about two years to recover, but your marriage can be stronger than it was before. The therapist you find may also be able to refer you to a support group for infidelity.

How to Take His Apology

If your partner wants to continue your relationship, he'll likely apologize very frequently, nearly every day. You may not accept his apology for a long time—maybe never—but it is a good sign if he continues to offer it.

Apologies and Your Religion

Some women will never accept an apology, because an affair is so contrary to her ethical or religious beliefs about marriage and the vows she has taken in a holy ceremony. She may be able to go on and to try to build a stronger marriage, but she may not ever be able to accept an apology and forgive. On the other hand, some women accept an apology *because* of a religious belief that one must forgive. Even if you accept his apology for religious reasons, both of you must understand why he had the affair, not only to help you heal, but to try to make your relationship as affair-proof as possible.

An Apology Is Not a Magic Wand

Regardless of when and if you choose to accept his apology, the affair does not just go away with disclosure and an apology and a promise not to do it again. You probably can't even accept his apology until you two complete the process of understanding this affair, in terms of what it means, and the harm it does. See Chapter 12 for more on apologies.

If the apology comes from a serial lover, he has already lost all credibility because of his history of having so many affairs. He must admit to his behavior and, depending on the situation, take whatever steps are necessary to end it. For example, if he is a sex addict, he must start treatment and commit to it, until there is resolution of his problem. This is why it is so important to understand the motivation for the affair beyond the sexuality. The sexuality is a quick fix, but it may not be the sole motivation. *To try to make the marriage affair-proof, the reason must be identified, so that the appropriate course of therapy is prescribed.* It is important that you both understand it and agree to it; then the road becomes smoother.

How You Feel about Yourself

Not only do you find yourself in shock from your partner's infidelity, but you probably are experiencing a drop in self-esteem. Why? You likely see his affair as mainly a sexual phenomenon, rather than his failure to cope with emotional issues. You also may look at yourself as a sexual being who has failed, as if you don't measure up in terms of beauty and sexuality. Women whose husbands have cheated feel that they are not pretty or desirable. You fantasize about their meetings and imagine that they are glamorous Hollywood sexual scenes (even though this is usually far from the case). You are afraid that you pale by comparison, and you believe you fall short in your relations with your spouse.

You also probably think the other woman must be a "knockout." Yet reports from men show that most of the time the other woman is **not** as attractive as his wife. Often she is not attractive at all, as many partners later attest. You, of course, have a hard time believing him. The truth is that the "other woman" is sometimes overweight and so far from glamorous that the wife cannot believe he wanted to have sex with her, let alone jeopardize their relationship for her.

IT'S NOT ABOUT HER LOOKS

If the other woman is not a glamour queen as the wife imagines, what attracts him? In most cases it's that she can provide sex in a quiet place without any of the concerns that a married couple has. The atmosphere is different, so he can relax and not have any duties to attend to or responsibilities to take care of *at that moment.* For him, the affair is an escape. The husband is using the excitement and sex with a woman other than his wife as a way to solve problems in his life and marriage.

Feeling Emotional Abandonment

While many men do not see the seriousness of the affair in the early stages and may even wonder if his partner is making too much of it, you most likely experience his infidelity as an emotional abandonment. You had trusted him to always be with you, for the two of you to be a team, to support one another and help each other, but in having an affair, he has thrown away this concept. You had built a history together and were looking to create a future together. It is abandonment—*but the destruction can be rebuilt.*

Specialness

What hits you the hardest when your partner has an affair is that you feel you have lost your place in his heart, and with that the feeling of "specialness" that you have always held. He had taken vows in front of witnesses that he would be faithful—your parents, family, and friends probably watched; perhaps you've had children together, celebrated special occasions, and suffered losses together and comforted each other. You two have a history, but you know he has taken another woman into his arms and desecrated those vows and understandings. Your partner now must help you reclaim the most important feeling that every woman wants in her marriage: *being his special one.* He must work hard at bringing you back to your rightful position. He must help you heal from this trauma, and then together, you must rebuild your lives.

How Much to Know about the Affair

In the first few months after the news hits, as you rebuild your life together, you will struggle with thoughts of his infidelity and wonder about what happened. You think of them together. Some women want to know every detail and others want to know nothing. If you learn *everything,* you may find you have images in your mind that haunt you and cause distress. For example, women who want to know the sexual details about the affair often find they cannot rid themselves of the images. Many experience difficulties when she and her partner start to have sex again and those images come to mind. There is a middle ground on what to know and what not to know.

Knowing certain things will help you understand what happened and what this affair means to your partner. Ask your partner these questions:

- Do you love me?
- Do you love the person with whom you are having an affair?
- Does she want to marry you?
- Have you given her up?
- If you haven't, why haven't you?
- How did you meet?
- Did she supply something that was missing between us?
- Can we capture what you found missing in our marriage?
- If so, what was it?
- Was it hard to give her up?
- Was there a point where you were planning to leave me?
- If so, what kept you from leaving?

The answers to these questions help you gauge how emotionally involved (if at all) your partner was in the affair, and how he feels about your future. Listen to not only the words he says, but how he says them. Does he appear engaged and honest? Is he sensitive to your feelings?

Your Partner's Reaction

Your partner's reaction to the infidelity is not like yours, of course, because he is not shocked and bewildered. You are out of sync because he has possessed this information for a while and has been processing it in silence. That means your adjustments will be different. Your partner's reaction can vary widely—from not confessing to the truth, to denying the truth or even having his buddies lie for him, to telling the truth. But typically, you discover it or are told about the infidelity. He is usually waiting to see what your reaction will be.

Most men report that they are shocked by their partner's reaction because it is much more severe than they had expected. Men don't anticipate the strength of a woman's reaction to the news. Though his shock is unsettling, know that it is common.

At this point, he must end the infidelity. Unfortunately, he doesn't always do this. If he continues and tells you it is over and it is not, the discovery of the second lie will have a very detrimental effect on the recovery process. The bottom line here is that *any other lies after the discovery of the affair will further erode the trust in the marriage.*

ACKNOWLEDGE HIS FEELINGS

Though you may not care about his feelings at this point, it's still important to acknowledge that you both have an emotional response to this situation. He may feel guilt and depression and you will feel, among many emotions, anger and depression. If in two weeks you do not experience a decrease in these emotions, you both must see a therapist or physician for evaluation.

Exercise

1. What information have you learned about your husband's reasons for having this affair?
2. Do you find any truth in the reasons your husband gave for his having an affair?
3. What have you learned about your husband's feeling for the other woman?
4. How do you feel about what you heard?
5. Does this information provide you with a plan of action?
6. Is your husband willing to work together with you on the feelings you have from the affair? Yes/No
7. Will he enter therapy with you to help resolve this issue? Yes/No
8. If he does not, will you see a therapist to help you through this transition? Yes/No

chapter eleven

COPING

SKILLS

The myriad reactions following discovery of an affair calls for a repertoire of skills to help you cope. This chapter covers the all-important skill of effective communication, and also discusses those related to anger and depression, cognitive therapy, self-nurturing behavior, and professional help. These skills can be easily learned, and mistakes that you make along the way as a beginner can be corrected.

Grief

The months after the initial discovery are filled with doubts and fears and reactions that are similar to grief reactions. You feel as though you have sustained a great loss; as one woman told me, "It was the innocence of my marriage." You will experience emotional pain that is devastating. Sometimes you feel rage so strong that you are frightened by it, and other days you feel depression so profound that you are immobilized. Eventually these emotions will decrease in intensity and you will be able to come to terms with what has happened. You may have sleep disturbances; either oversleeping or not being able to sleep enough. The same is true for eating, maybe eating too much or not eating enough. As you continue reading, you will find ways to help you cope and to become stronger.

Obsessive Review

As you process the infidelity, you will likely be most disturbed by the phenomenon of *obsessive review* described by psychiatrist Robert Weiss. It is the nonstop thinking about what has happened, repeatedly going over what you know, and trying to find answers to what you don't know. It seems that you have no control over when and how often these thoughts enter your mind, and you think you must be going crazy. *You are not going crazy.* You will have flashbacks to times when you saw them together or he spoke in a way that puzzled you. This obsessive review is a way to internalize what has happened and to make it part of your history.

Joan, who had recently learned of her husband's infidelity, said in her support group, *I've never experienced anything like this. I must be going crazy. I can't stop thinking and thinking about it. It is like I am a prisoner of my thoughts.*

Other women in the group nodded in agreement. You must be assured you are not going crazy, but having a reaction to a trauma. More and more therapists are beginning to think of infidelity as a trauma. To understand this, think back to September 11, 2001, when the United States went through the traumatic experience of being under terrorist attack. We could not stop watching the television screen. We were all conducting an obsessive review of what transpired.

Knowing that the obsessive review is normal should give you reassurance that it will eventually go away, but in the meantime, there are some things you can do to help yourself cope with it.

Coping with the Obsessive Review

Though it is normal to think about your husband's infidelity as much as you do, you still need to learn to control your obsessive review. Believe it or not, you can control when and how much you will think. Decide on a time when you will not be disturbed and allow yourself to think of the affair for thirty minutes. Think of whatever you want, *but do not exceed the time you allot for this exercise.* Pick a start time, set the alarm for a half hour, and allow yourself to think. Then, when that time is over, *stop thinking.* Go on to do something else. It is easier to stop when you have something specific to do afterward, like meeting a friend or gardening. In the beginning, soon after the discovery, you will probably need to plan frequent thinking sessions, and then decrease your schedule, from five times a week to three and so on, as well as reducing the time allotted for obsessing. As Scarlett O'Hara said in *Gone with the Wind,* "I'll think about that tomorrow." One day, you *will* forget the review, and that is good. It won't be long before you won't need the timed sessions.

When you find yourself obsessing outside of your allotted time, do something to stop it. You can try thought-stopping techniques, like wearing a rubber band on your wrist and snapping it, popping a mint in your mouth, making a phone call, or splashing cold water on your face. This is a signal to you to stop obsessing. It is much like Pavlov's dog, who learned to salivate when he heard the bell. You will learn to stop your thinking when you pop that mint in your mouth or snap the rubber band.

Talk Time

"Talk Time" is a scheduled time to meet with your partner to discuss the questions you have about his infidelity. The reason for doing this is to keep the tone at home more even and "safe" and to prevent assailing him with accusations at other times. You will feel better knowing that you have time to be heard and to have your questions answered, and he will feel better and be more relaxed if he knows *when* you will be raising your concerns.

Talk time should be done two or three times a week shortly after the discovery of the affair and less frequently as the anger in the home subsides. Limit total time to one hour; you cannot solve all problems in one evening. Meet at the same time and day of the week every week. Make this meeting "top priority" or "sacred" time for the two of you.

Guidelines for Talk Time

- No interruptions allowed (with the exception of emergencies).
- Come prepared with your topic for discussion.
- The first person speaks, using an "I" message (to be discussed later in this chapter). Take turns starting, and agree to alternate who starts unless one of you announces a pressing need to begin.
- Next, the partner repeats the statement. This assures the other that the message is received and understood.
- Then you can go on to problem-solving.
- Each person gets about fifteen minutes to deal with his or her particular issue. Use a timer or clock so that you won't start arguing about procedure.
- Then the other one gets the next fifteen minutes, and so on. Again, do not meet for more than an hour.

- Do not defend yourself when your partner is talking. *This part of the meeting is for understanding your partner. Your job is to listen and try to understand.*
- If things are **not** going well, it may be best to postpone your discussion until later by asking for a time-out. This concept must be agreed upon in advance so that neither of you takes offense. A time-out is different from walking out on someone; that feels like abandonment. The couple simply agrees to pick up the conversation at a different time when they are feeling more relaxed. Say something like: *Tom, I need a time-out. Let's talk again tomorrow night at eight. Is this okay with you?*
- If time ends before you have answered all the questions, put those questions aside for the next meeting. If you have a particular question that causes a lot of disagreement, you may also put that aside for the next session.

Family Meetings

When your life settles down and you and your husband have made infidelity a part of your history, I suggest you start another type of meeting called the Family Meeting. The rules are pretty similar, but the changes are that the children are invited and the topic changes to family issues. It is not a time to discuss infidelity. Use the time for everyone to have a chance to bring up a concern that may be bothering them, plan time for the family to do things together, the parents plan their time out together, and chores are assigned. Teach your children to use "I messages" and you will see democracy working in your own home and the kids will learn a lot they can use in their futures both with friends, on the job, and when they marry.

Coping with Anger

Anger is an uncomfortable emotion to deal with because it affects you both emotionally and physically. From the moment you discover that your husband has been involved with another woman, your body and mind dwell on this most uncomfortable experience. The anger you feel can be the result of the underlying issues related to the affair, and may also indicate a power struggle between you and your partner.

EMOTIONAL TURMOIL

Anger is only one emotion couples face after an affair. There are others, but they are not immediately recognized because of the impact of the startling news and the overwhelming response of anger. Anger is what I consider a cover-up emotion. It happens quickly, but hidden behind that reaction are the powerful feelings of hurt, betrayal, and especially abandonment. These are many of the emotions attended to in therapy.

Anger is like a fuel and it must be burned off in some way. Effective communication can help defuse some of the anger, and some ineffective communication can increase anger. However, there are other means of decreasing anger. You can find some relief in physical exercise, relaxation, and cognitive areas. Following are self-help skills that you can call upon at almost any time to help yourself deal with anger.

Exercise

You can first try to burn off anger through exercise. Regularly scheduled exercise helps, because the body responds with increased endorphins that will make you feel better. Over the years, many women have told me what has helped them. One told me she kept a stack of old magazines or newspapers and tore them to shreds when she felt angry. Another used a punching bag; still another swung her child's *Star Wars* light saber into the gut of her imagined husband; and a third punched pillows (however, some people find their anger *increased* with punching pillows).

What you choose is up to you, as long as it is helpful and accessible. The goal is to relax your muscles and make you feel calmer. An excellent and simple exercise is walking. If you find a friend to join you, you will be less likely to find excuses not to exercise, and, as so many women have told me, they looked forward to the walk with their friend (and sometimes they ended it with a coffee at a nearby shop).

Relaxation Techniques

Anger brings tension to all parts of your body and this is not healthy, especially when you are angry week after week. Thus, it is important to find ways to cope with anger. If you have established a way to relax, I suggest you use it regularly. If you have not, you can try the following.

Preparation for Relaxation

- Pick a time when you will not be interrupted. Allow voice mail to pick up your messages. Tell your family what you are planning to do and ask for their cooperation in not disturbing you.
- Set a schedule if possible. Same time, same place. Allow fifteen minutes.
- Wear comfortable clothing.
- Sit in a comfortable chair, but lie down if you can.
- Make the lighting in the room comfortable.

Relaxation Exercise

Take a deep breath, close your eyes and think of some very peaceful scene. You can see yourself floating on the water with the sun comfortably warming you, or you can picture yourself walking in a beautiful meadow with wildflowers around you, or you can be watching colorful balloons floating in the sky. Take in the beautiful scene, just relax, and enjoy. Don't rush. When you are ready to leave this lovely scene, wiggle your toes, stretch your arms, sit up, and go on with your day, a more rested and comfortable you.

Nurture Yourself

Above all, you must nurture and care for yourself as you work through your feelings about his infidelity. The way you do this is to consciously take actions **every day** to make yourself feel better. What you do depends on what you like. Play music that you love. Remember to eat well; cook favorite meals for yourself. When you need help, ask for it. Reach out to others by calling a friend to talk or visiting someone; exercise, walk, work on a hobby, go to a movie, or watch TV.

Treat yourself to a relaxing bath by candlelight, with fragrant bath accessories.

Sometimes going out to the mall can be a distraction. However, do not drive if you are angry. Call a friend and see if she will pick you up so you can go to the mall, a museum, or to take in a movie.

What you don't want to do is sit around and cry, drink, use drugs, or overeat. This mood will not last forever—you will ride it out.

Journaling

Another way to deal with anger is to write down your thoughts in a private and personal journal. Writing helps reduce anger by letting it out and it helps you see how far you have come when you look back to revisit where you have been. Your journal should be private and for your eyes only. You will feel better from writing a journal. It seems simple, but don't dismiss it. Some women say it is the best way to release pain and that it becomes an important part of what they do each day.

The Unmailed Letter

Writing a letter to your husband expressing your feelings will help release the anger that is locked in you. *However, do not show this letter to anyone, and absolutely not to your husband. It is a therapeutic exercise only.* When you know you are not restricted by any rules and can use the letter to blow off steam, you will not censor yourself; you will, instead, release your anger. Write your letter in an unrestricted manner because *it is for your eyes only*. Keep it locked away after writing it.

Rituals

Later, when this ordeal is over, you can destroy that letter in a way that is therapeutic for you. It can symbolize the end of the affair. You might decide to tear it up into pieces and burn it or flush it away. Another way is to take the letter to a stream or body of water, tear it in little pieces, and throw each piece in the water. Let the water wash it away. Then, go out to a special place for dinner with your husband for a private little ceremony. You can tell him that you have turned the corner and are looking forward to a new and wonderful life together with the affair behind you both. This is actually a ritual, which is a way we signify the end of something and the beginning of something else. Destroying your letter and flushing it away is like ending the past hurts, and having the dinner together is a way to the new beginning. (Again: Don't read him the letter.) Don't tell him about the letter or discuss the affair. Talk about future plans, that you are feeling better, and that you are closing the door on this affair. You will begin to feel free of this burden.

Cognitive Therapy

You feel the way you think you feel. If you continue to think angry thoughts, it's likely that you'll continue to feel angry. It is possible to reduce anger by understanding the thought process you are using that may be contributing to this. You can challenge your thoughts and see them mirrored in the way you feel. The way you do this is through *cognitive therapy*, which gives you a way to help yourself without assistance from anyone else. Cognitive therapy can help you identify and change dysfunctional thinking, behavior, and emotional responses. It shows you how to challenge the distortion that depresses you and replace it with positive thoughts, whether you think them, say them, or someone says them to you. I will show you three ways of using this concept to challenge your thinking. Let's start with distortions in thinking.

Distortions in Thinking

The following ten distortions are listed in the book *Feeling Good* by Dr. David Burns, a leader in the field of cognitive therapy. These concepts are a very effective treatment for the negative thoughts and emotions that have been disturbing you since the discovery of your husband's infidelity. It will help you with your anger, depression, and drop in self-esteem. In these examples, I'll explain the distorted thought and give an example of its use. Following each is a statement that challenges the distortion and shows another way of thinking that is not distorted. This concept can be applied to many situations, not just the aftermath of infidelity. You may even realize that you tend to use one or more distortions on a regular basis. If so, understanding them and being observant about how you use them will help you now and in your future. Let's apply Dr. Burns's cognitive distortions to your situation.

1. All-or-Nothing Thinking

This describes a way of looking at situations in the extremes. It is sometimes called "black-or-white thinking." It does not allow for moderation.

Distortion: Because he cheated on me once, I can never trust him again.

Change to: Because he cheated once does not necessarily mean he will do it again. I will have to work with him and bring in safeguards that show me it will not happen again.

You can see how despair can be changed to hope, minimizing the pain.

2. Overgeneralization

This occurs when a person takes one event and applies it to include everything.

Distortion: I realize that he is just a big playboy kind of guy and I don't feel I can trust him.

Change to: He admits he made a big mistake. That doesn't mean he is a womanizer. It means he made this mistake, which he promises will never happen again. We will have to work with each other to build up trust.

In the change of statement, the individual does not wipe out her future by saying that one behavior will always apply in the future.

3. Mental Filter

This happens when one event among many is focused on and all others lose significance.

Distortion: I think of the lies he told me and I can't believe him anymore.
Change to: He also has been honest in the past. He is remorseful. I will be careful, but I must give him a chance. I can't just always think of the deceit.

4. Disqualifying the Positive

This refers to a pessimistic reading of positive events that happen. You believe they just don't count. "Beginner's luck" is an example of the way many positive attributes can quickly be discounted.

Distortion: He's acting very sweet, but I think he just does what the therapist tells him to do.
Change to: Maybe he is being sweet because he wants to make me feel better and because he is sorry for what he has done. Even if he does it because the therapist told him to, he is changing his behavior.

5. Mind Reading/Fortunetelling

Making an assumption about someone's behavior or motivation and not checking it out with that person puts you in the category of mind reader.

Distortion: I can see him looking at women when we are out. He must be imagining himself in bed with them.
Change to: I don't know what he thinks. I will have to ask him.

Related to this is predicting the future. This is also referred to as "fortunetelling."

Distortion: I will never be able to trust John again.

Change to: John is willing to work with me on trust. I must allow for time to build trust again. This is the first time in twenty years he has broken my trust.

Fortunetelling is based on the same principle as mind reading because it involves coming to conclusions without any evidence to support them. However, when you state your thoughts correctly, your future looks more promising. This is not denying reality. You are not tricking yourself; you are using rational thinking. You can see how this tactic will lower emotional reactivity and decrease the feeling of hopelessness, because you have identified a starting point for change.

6. Magnification/Minimization

This is a distortion that takes a sledgehammer to your self-esteem by magnifying your errors and minimizing your achievements.

Distortion: I couldn't see the clues while it was happening.
Change to: I didn't want to see the clues. I must concentrate now on better communication in our relationship.

Distortion: Everyone will think that I wasn't a good enough wife.
Change to: I am making a big deal over what everyone else thinks and I really don't know what people think. I need to concentrate on our relationship and what *we* think.

7. Emotional Reasoning

This distortion refers to the tendency to attribute conclusions to the way you feel. It is a really important distortion to recognize and give up if you have been using it.

Distortion: I feel like a failure. So I must be a failure. He seemed so in love with me that I did not think he would have an affair.
Change to: Because I feel that way doesn't make it true. I am not a failure because my husband had an affair.

8. "Should" Statement

This distortion sets standards that you compare behavior to, whether it is yours or someone else's. It can lead to guilt when regret would do as well.

Distortion: I should have seen how the other men in his family treated women.
Change to: Even if I had noticed, it is not a guarantee that he would behave in the same or different way.

This is an important distortion to recognize, so that you can talk about it with him and ask him questions if you need to.

9. Labeling and Mislabeling

This amounts to a one-word critique that does not allow a deeper and more accurate description of a person or an event. Rather than label, describe the situation.

Distortion: I was such an idiot not to recognize what was going on with him and Sondra.
Change to: I am not to blame for not recognizing their affair.

Remember, people having an affair do their best to keep it a secret.

10. Personalization

This is a distortion in which a person sees herself as responsible for events that were not her fault.

Distortion: I am not pretty enough to have kept my husband's interest.
Change to: Men do not have an affair because the woman is prettier.

Men often have affairs with women who are not as pretty as their wife. They have affairs for other reasons, many of which have nothing to do with you.

Remind Yourself

I suggest you copy these distortions and put them up on your refrigerator door, where you will always see them. I have asked women in my *Surviving Infidelity* groups to do this, and the reports back were excellent. Many came to recognize that they use one or two distortions more than others. Just as this has helped them, it will help you to change your outlook, and, thus, your negative emotions.

Rational Thinking

The second method of making you aware of what you are thinking was introduced by Albert Ellis, one of the first psychologists to recognize the power of our thoughts on our emotions, who developed Rational Emotive Behavior Therapy. He presented the equation $A + B = C$, with A being the objective *activating act*, B being the subjective *belief*, and C being the *consequences* (an emotional response). Finally, there is D, which is where you challenge or *dispute* your belief system.

A = **Activating Act:** what happened
B = **Belief:** your belief about what happened
C = **Consequences:** how you feel now
D = **Dispute:** dispute your "belief"

Let's look at an example to see how it works.

A = **Activating Act:** At a wedding party for my neighbor's daughter, I saw a young woman flirting with Terry and I became nervous.
B = **Belief:** Your belief is that Terry will be attracted to women that he meets.
C = **Consequences:** Your anxiety increases by such a belief.
D = **Dispute** (you must **Dispute** the **Belief**): I can't stop someone from flirting with Terry. He and I are recovering from a marital crisis and I am ever-vigilant. This will slowly subside as I build trust.

Let's try another example:

A = Activating Act: I was afraid to have sex with Terry last night.

B = Belief: This is huge. We can't recover from this.

C = Consequences: You feel anxious.

D = Dispute: I liked sex with Terry before and we will work to recover that just as we have worked on all of our issues to date. Right now I am too angry. As I deal with working through the issues, our sex life will return.

Correlation

There is a correlation between Dr. Burns's concept and that of Dr. Ellis. You can use Dr. Burns's distortions to challenge **B**, Dr. Ellis's belief system. So if you are trying to understand your emotions (**C**) and what you are thinking (**B**), look back at the ten distortions in thinking. Then you will discover the meaning of what you are saying to yourself and will be able to arrive at **D**. See if your mood doesn't change when you do.

Checking the Evidence

A third way to cope with negative thoughts (those that make you sad, depressed, anxious, or frightened) is by checking evidence to see if you are really correct in your thinking. This concept was introduced by noted psychiatrist Aaron Beck, who founded the Beck Institute for Cognitive Therapy and Research and is considered by many to be the father of cognitive therapy. This is a simple, excellent method that you can use anywhere, immediately after you have a negative thought. Here is what to do:

1. Be aware of your feelings. (Awareness)
2. If your feeling is uncomfortable, identify it (as depressing, anxiety-producing, angry, jealous, and so on). (Emotion)
3. After that, recall what you were thinking. (Thought)
4. Ask yourself this question: What evidence is there for that? That is how you check out whether or not your thought is irrational. (Evidence)

For example, Janet is working on her garden and she begins to feel sad (Emotion). She stops working to check out her thoughts (Awareness). She remembers she was thinking that her husband, Sam, told her that he would be late for dinner because he had a quick meeting after work. She began to think that he was going to see Molly, the woman he had had an affair with (Thought). She asked herself what the evidence was, but couldn't find any. She knew he had not seen Molly for three months; he had been very loving and attentive; the meeting was, as he described it, quick; and she knew it must be related to the big conference his firm was planning. She felt better after checking out the evidence, but she decided, nevertheless, to check it out with Sam when he returned home.

Understanding Rationalization

Rationalization is a way to deceive oneself about behavior that is harmful. This is different from **rational thinking**, which is thinking clearly about the consequences of your actions. **Rationalization** is making excuses for your actions. Rationalization is an unconscious defense mechanism to protect yourself or someone else from the truth and the pain of one's behavior. The following are ways in which people try to fool themselves and others, followed by the ways to refute the rationalizing. So if your partner tries to rationalize his behavior while explaining his affair, you can refute it.

Rationalization: I thought you would never know.
Refute: Even if I never knew, it is not the right thing to do. No one knows what I might accidentally find out. But that is not the point. It is what is right and what is wrong.

Rationalization: I thought what you didn't know wouldn't hurt you.
Refute: But I did know. One way or another, I felt something was wrong. You were cheating me of a full marital and family life, and that feels terrible.

Rationalization: I am sorry I did it, but all your needs are met. Nothing in your life has changed. So what's the big deal?

Refute: The big deal is that I have lost respect for you and no longer trust you.

When faced with uncomfortable facts, people often resort to rationalization to minimize or deny the true facts of the situation. If someone says something to you that hurts, you can reply that it is hurtful, but you can also think about the remark at a later time by yourself, with a confidant, your support group, or your therapist. It may be you were speaking to someone who does not recognize your pain. You do not have to accept what was said; you can refute it. When you are stronger, you can refute it on the spot if you choose.

Communication

Communicating effectively is different from just talking without shouting at each other. A major key to communicating effectively is listening, really listening. Listening to what the other person is saying is only half the job, however. The other half is to *let the person know you hear and understand* what is being said. As you move forward during the postaffair period, effective communication is more important than ever. You both need to learn from the affair, and it's vital to keep the lines of communication open as you do that.

How to Start Effective Communication

Chances are good that your communication as a couple was not healthy prior to the affair. You may not have talked at all, or may have argued a lot. *Communication that hurts individuals also shows that the marriage is hurting and is in trouble.* Dr. John Gottman, psychologist and cofounder and codirector of the Gottman Institute, called such negative communication the "Four Horsemen of the Apocalypse." These Four Horsemen are *criticism, contempt, defensiveness*, and *stonewalling*. By remembering these four words, you will understand when the communication you use or that someone else directs at you can easily lead to trouble. The following guidelines will help you avoid these pitfalls.

1. The "I" Message

Use an "I" message whenever possible to begin the process of communication. You start with "I" and say what is troubling you, how you feel about it, and if possible, what you would like to have done about it. The purpose of the "I" message is that it will keep you from using an accusatory opening with a "harsh start-up" as Dr. Gottman so aptly named it.

Here's an example of using the "I" message: *When you work late, I worry about what it could mean, and so I want you to call and tell me what is going on.*

Then the second person makes a statement in reply, which is really a repetition of the "I" message. This reply shows empathy even if the person doesn't agree with it. (Later in the conversation, it will become resolved.) The following illustrations show the difference between a harsh start-up and a softer one using the "I" message. When you say "I" rather than "you," you are taking responsibility for your feelings and are not blaming the other person.

Accusatory: It really pisses me off when you hide behind that paper all evening.
Change to "I" message: I feel ignored when we don't talk to each other in the evening.

Accusatory: You make all the decisions in the family.
Change to "I" message: I feel I don't get any input on our decisions.

Accusatory: You don't act like you are attracted to me.
Change to "I" message: I feel so sad because I think you are no longer attracted to me.

Accusatory: You are infuriating when it comes to making love. You have all the say.
Change to "I" message: I feel that I am ignored along with my needs when it comes to sex.

2. Replying with Empathy

When someone replies to an "I" message, it will most likely be with empathy. If that happens, the person who begins a conversation with the "I" message knows that she has been heard and that her partner knows what she was feeling. This is a major concept in effective communication. To illustrate the use of empathy, let us take the previous statements and give an empathetic reply.

Wife ("I" message): I feel ignored when you read the paper all evening.
Husband (answering with empathy): *You are feeling I am not as interested in you as I am in the paper.*

Wife ("I" message): I feel I don't get any input on our decisions.
Husband (answering with empathy): You feel I take charge of everything and don't ask for input from you.

Wife ("I" message): I feel so sad because I think you are no longer attracted to me.
Husband (answering with empathy): You are feeling that you no longer attract me.

Wife ("I" message): I feel that I am ignored along with my needs when it comes to sex.
Husband (answering with empathy): You think I don't think of your sexual needs.

When you start the conversation with an "I" message, you set the tone for a conversation **without** accusations. It may seem to you that in each case the reply to an "I" message is a repetition. *It is*—because at this step, repeating the message will let the other person know that she is really being heard. Being heard is a key to good communication. In the aftermath of the affair, a great deal of anger and nasty accusations are thrown about. This will decrease with the "I" message, since it eliminates the accusatory opening. When he responds with empathy, it indicates to you that he is not denying your experience. This will help defuse anger.

"I" messages, which tell another person how you feel and what you would like to have happen, are not to be confused with the **"I" statements** we talked about earlier, on page 120. They are statements about your core values and something you could never do. They are usually a response.

Example #1:

CHUCK: *Honey, I know a club we can go to where we can swing with other couples. They have bars, TV, music; and it's supposed to be lots of fun. Then couples pair off. Next visit, you meet a new couple.*
CYNTHIA: *I will never participate in that kind of thing, ever. Don't ask me. I am furious. (Core value)*

Example #2:

JACK: *Bob and Jane want us to join them at their swingers club.*
CAROLE: *That may be fun for them, but I will never do that. (Core value)*

Example #3

HENRY: *Let's skip Christmas at your mother's and go skiing.*
BEA: *I will never skip Christmas at my mother's house. It's a family tradition that I value. (Core value)*

The following example shows **ineffective communication** and, therefore, no resolution.

HE: *I told you a thousand times I am NEVER going to see her again. I learned my lesson. What else do you want?*
SHE: *I don't know. I really don't know.*
HE: *Then what do you want, for heaven's sake? I can't help what happened.*

SHE: *You could have. You could have kept your fly zipped!*

The following is **effective** communication:

SHE: *I think you're in bed with her when you change your plans and don't tell me.*
HE: *When I change my plans, it worries you that I am not being faithful?*
SHE: *Yes. I feel I can't trust you.*
HE: *I understand that you can't trust me. What can I do?*
SHE: *Tell me when you change your plans, and continue not seeing her.*
HE: *You want proof?*
SHE: *Yeah, sure. Good idea.*
HE: *I will call you and tell you when plans change.*
SHE: *That doesn't happen much, and I still worry.*
HE: *If you don't know for sure what I am doing, you worry?*
SHE: *Yes.*
HE: *Then I will call you much more often and tell you what I am doing and what is going on. Will that help?*
SHE: *Yes, very much. Thank you.*
HE: *Now I understand.*

The last examples show how starting with an "I" message and continuing with empathy leads to solutions rather than defensiveness. The opposite of the "I" message is pointing a finger and then beginning with "you." A start-up like this will cause the communication to go downhill. Every time you say something nasty, the chance of good communication decreases, while the chance for an argument increases.

3. Denying Another's Experience

When you deny the other person's experience, you will most likely make him angry. Communication declines and anger rises. When a person tells you how he feels, that is a true statement of his perception.

It doesn't matter if you think he shouldn't feel that way or think it is ridiculous for him to feel that way. It is his reality, and denying it will cut off communication. So what do you do? You recognize it, and let him know you understand it. It does not mean you agree with his statement.

Example: Ineffective communication

BILL: *I don't know why I did it. I don't know what came over me.*
CYNTHIA: *"You don't know why you did it." Do you expect me to believe that lame excuse? You were hot for her. That's what came over you.*
BILL: *What's the use? You can't understand anything.*

Example: Effective communication

ROB: *I don't know why I did it. I don't know what came over me.*
CAROLE: *You had an affair, but you don't know why.*
ROB: *It sounds lame, like a poor excuse, but I don't really know why I did something that I am so ashamed of. I would do anything to turn back the clock.*
CAROLE: *We can't do that, but I am willing to listen if you tell me the truth.*
ROB: *I will.*

Tips for Good Communication

- **Avoid "why" questions.** Do not ask a question starting with "why," because it often sounds accusatory and puts the other person on the defensive. Instead, ask him to explain, tell you, or walk you through his decision-making process.
  Examples:
  Why: Why did you pick a friend of mine to have the affair?
  Use instead: Explain your thinking in picking my friend for the affair.
  Why: Why did you lie to my parents about where you went when you were with her?

Use instead: Tell me how you decided to tell my parents where you were on that trip.

Why: Why didn't you get me an anniversary gift this year?

Use instead: What made you decide not to get me an anniversary gift this year?

- *Do not use absolutes.* Absolutes are words like *never, always, all the time,* and *only.* Cousins in these categories are *ought, should have,* and *must.* There are very few situations that can be described in absolutes, and when someone uses absolutes incorrectly, anger increases.

Examples:
  - *You* never *give me any surprises.*
  - *You* always *think of yourself first.*
  - *You* should have *considered us.*

- **Describe the situation.** Rather than using absolutes, accusations, and sentences that inflame the anger, describe what has happened.

  Inflammatory: You told everyone in the car pool about the affair and now your mother knows and called up screaming. How could you be so stupid? Call her.

  Descriptive: Your mother knows about the affair and is crying. I think you'd better call her before we have dinner.

- **Use appropriate body language.** Poor body language conveys an attitude of aggression (or other emotions) rather than one of reaching out for a solution. Standing with your hand on your hip, crossing your arms over your chest, or waving your finger are signs of aggression.

- **Don't speak in phrases that will make your partner angry.** Examples are, "Yeah, right," "Oh, sure," "Whatever you say." These indicate lying or disinterest. If you think he is not telling the truth, tell him, using an "I" message.

- **Consider your tone of voice.** The appropriate voice tone will invite a reasonable response. Do not talk over a person or shout. Your voice can convey anger, fear, nonbelief, and other emotions as well. It can also register a willingness to listen and cooperate.

- **Maintain good eye contact.** Proper eye contact is respectful and will lead to a willingness to listen. Not looking at the person can register deceit, guilt, or contempt. Rolling your eyes when the other is speaking shows contempt and is a real conversation stopper. It will understandably increase his anger toward you.
- **Talk at an appropriate time.** If you want to talk at a time other than the scheduled Talk Time, be sure it is a good time for your partner. Ask him if it is, and if he says "no," ask for a time when it will be okay.
- **Rehearse before talking about a hot topic.** If you feel anxious about bringing up a particular topic, conduct a mental rehearsal as described by Maxwell Maltz in his book *Psycho-Cybernetics*. Use relaxation exercises to help you relax. Then have a "mental" rehearsal in which you try out different ways in which you will ask your question, imagine different responses, and try out ways to reply to the responses. You will desensitize yourself to the anxiety of the situation and, thus, be more relaxed when it occurs.

Professional Help

A therapist who has had experience in working with infidelity can help guide you through this difficult time. There are many bumps on the road to recovery, and having a guide is important. It takes a long time to reach your goal, so you will likely need this guide—someone in the mental health field, such as a psychiatrist, psychologist, marriage and family therapist, or social worker. Be sure the therapist is licensed and experienced. A therapist is obligated to tell you this; if he or she doesn't, ask. Essentially, therapy is talking with someone who is not emotionally involved in your problem, who will listen to what you are saying, and discuss it with you. You and your husband will work together with the therapist, who will help you both understand how the situation evolved and help you through the anger and other difficult emotions that you are experiencing.

One of the benefits of therapy is that the intimacy between you and your husband will grow because you are speaking honestly to each other. Maybe for the first time, you see life from the other's viewpoint, and then begin to understand more deeply what has happened and why. You see your patterns and realize they are the sum of all your experiences: family, work, desires, and goals. You will form a deeper sense of intimacy than you probably have ever had. This intimacy will continue, and, most important, you will have the skills to handle any future concerns.

An additional help would be belonging to a support group led by a licensed mental health professional. Search in your area to find one.

Exercise

1. Look through Dr. Burns's ten cognitive distortions and find three that you use frequently. Write down an example of those three and then refute them.

   Distortion 1:

   Refute:

   Distortion 2:

   Refute:

   Distortion 3:

   Refute:

2. Write down a thought that makes you anxious. Using Dr. Ellis's A + B = C formula, fill out the equation and then Dispute it with D.

   A:

   B:

   C:

   D:

3. Plan out your week now, finding time for yourself and time to follow the suggestions in this chapter.

chapter twelve

LOOKING FORWARD

This last chapter shows you how to bring your husband into the process of helping in your healing and to find more ways to help the two of you re-establish and strengthen the bond that you have. If you've read this far, you likely have decided to try to work on your relationship rather than end it immediately, and you know that you do have a chance of healing and moving forward with your life together.

Your decision depends in part on where you see your husband on the continuum according to outcomes, the type of affair he is having, what stage his affair is in, your resources, the assets in your marriage in comparison to the deficits (as we discussed about affairs due to transitions in life, and how you might solve the marital problems that you find underlying the affair). These important choices need to be made using rational thinking along with the help of your therapist, who can assess your progress and guide you to your goal.

You are in the process of healing as you move forward from a difficult time. Every day, you will make progress, even though you will have bad days amidst the good. When you bring your husband into your healing process, you are joining your efforts to rebuild your marriage. Ask him to read this last chapter even if he has not read the rest of the book. He may find that helping you to heal helps him in his recovery as well.

Husband as Healer

You are both starting down a road to repair your relationship and to keep it free from further threats. Cheating on one's wife is the ultimate betrayal in a marriage. If your partner takes on this role of healer, it is an indication that he is trying to make amends and is doing it in a **relevant** way. Even if you are still angry at him, you do need his help at this difficult point in your relationship. The following are signs that he is on the path to healing your relationship and himself as well.

Did He End the Affair?

The first and most important action is for him *to end the affair* and promise never to see the other woman again. He should clearly express this to the affair person. This means he **cannot** contact her by phone, e-mail, text messages, regular mail, or by messenger. It's important that you know that his effort is sincere, so ask him how he ended the affair.

If the other woman resists the breakup, *he must tell her that there will be no more contact now or in the future.* There should **not** be a last meeting if at all possible. He also should tell her that you know about the affair. One of the ways you can be assured that your partner is trying to rebuild trust is if he tells you about any attempts she makes to contact him and how he handled each.

Your partner may insist on a last meeting because he feels guilty about how he has hurt his lover. Regardless, this meeting should **not** take place. It gives the affair person an opportunity to try to change his mind about his decision to stay with you.

THE LAST MEETING

If your partner feels strongly that he must see the affairee to say goodbye in person, make sure they meet in a public place, have a time limit of an hour, and do not go anywhere else. Ask him to call you when the meeting is over and then to come right home. Be aware that this is an opportunity for a second lie. A second lie tends to destroy the trust you and your partner are trying to rebuild. You will lose ground and lose any trust that has been rebuilt if he is dishonest about either the content or specifics of this meeting.

Is He Being Patient?

The greatest gift your partner can give you now is patience. The discovery of his affair is a trauma that can cause anxiety, flashbacks, nightmares, fear, sleep disturbances, anger, "startle reactions," and obsessive thinking. One of the most disturbing reactions is the obsessive review (see Chapter 11). As a result of thinking about it, you may respond with anger at almost any time. It seems to your partner that this anger comes from "out of the blue." Things will not change overnight, and it will take time for you to stop obsessing. He should not deny your experience, but admit to his behavior and apologize, even though he may already have done that many times. It would show a lack of patience and understanding if he were to yell back at you, even though you are calling him names, have done so repeatedly, and most likely will do it many times again. Your anger *will* subside over time, and the new skills you learned in Chapter 11 will help you manage these outbursts. Look for the following kinds of replies to your outbursts:

- *I agree with what you are saying about me and I am sorry. I apologize and will never do that again.*
- *I am sorry for what I did. I hurt you and I know it.*
- *I can't undo it. I wish I could, but I am so very sorry.*

He Writes Down His Thoughts

If your husband or partner writes down his thoughts in a love letter to you, you have something tangible to read when you are angry or depressed, or when he is not present. I strongly suggest you ask your partner to do this. Often after an affair, you will be wondering if your partner does really love you as he said he did or if he is thinking of the affair person. At such a time, when you are alone and plagued with doubts and fears, *reading that letter can help you.*

He can write of the first time he saw you, or recall pleasant past scenes, your attributes, and the qualities he loves you for.

If he is remorseful and wants to help you over this hurdle, you will have a love letter that you can read when all the doubts start to haunt you and the memories return.

Many men do not like to write, but they should make the attempt. If he finds he just can't write, he can buy a card that expresses his thoughts.

DON'T FORCE HIM

If he just cannot write a sincere love letter or buy a card, *he shouldn't do it; don't force him.* If he has **not** truly given up the affair, writing a love letter for you to read is only more deceit. It would be a second lie.

Rebuilding Trust

After an affair, rebuilding a sense of trust is a most challenging task. Your partner must understand that his *trust account* is down to zero and he must start to build it up. It won't just happen by itself; he must continue to make deposits to the account.

Signs That He Is Trying to Rebuild Trust

Rather than wait for you to ask what he has been doing, he should tell you. If you find a suspicious item on a credit card, he must explain what it is, even if it was for a night with the other woman. If he hears from the other woman, if he sees her, if he works late, if he has any unexplained absences, he must bring it up and explain what happened. If he is forthcoming, you can begin to trust him again, so you won't have to interrogate him, which neither of you likes.

If His Affair Was with a Coworker

If his affair was with a coworker, it is even harder to rebuild trust because he sees her every day and they may have to work late or go on trips together. He should try to make a big deposit in that trust account by explaining where he is at all times, calling you frequently, and arranging for you to call him, not necessarily on his cell phone, but on a land-based phone so you know where he is.

A thorny issue arises at office gatherings because others in the office are usually aware of the affair. It then becomes your partner's job at these occasions to say a brief hello to the other woman, not to ignore her but to be attentive to you, stay with you, smile, and send the little messages like a touch or an arm around you to signal others where his interest lies. Needless to say, he should not discuss the affair with anyone in the office. If he already has, he should back off and in a brief way let them know that it is over and he is not talking about it.

Dealing with Anniversaries

Anniversaries are emotional remembrances that your unconscious remembers before you do. On the anniversary of sad events or some days before, you may find yourself feeling blue. You may be alarmed, thinking that you are becoming depressed. You may become concerned because you have not been getting that depressed lately. This kind of anniversary can mark the date you found out about the affair, or any significant time related to both of you and the affair. Understand where it is coming from, tell your partner, and treat yourself and everyone else kindly. It is a time for self-nurturing and spending the evening doing something you both enjoy. The negative emotions will soon subside.

What Is an Appropriate Apology?

Although he has likely been apologizing ever since the discovery, the apology means most when it is offered near the end of therapy, when he has listened carefully and really understands what this has meant to you. It means more than an apology for just having been caught. In an appropriate apology, he feels remorse and expresses it. He also **must** understand your reaction and tell you precisely what he is sorry for.

The appropriate apology recognizes what the affair has cost you emotionally, expresses his remorse, and includes a promise never to be unfaithful in the future. Here are some samples of apologies and their "grade":

- **Grade A:** *I am sorry for the pain this caused you—your sleepless nights, your anxiety, your inability to eat, the migraines you suffered, and the embarrassment. Most of all, I caused you the loss of faith and trust you had in me. I hurt you and the children, which is inexcusable. I am mortified to see the pain in our parents' faces. I appreciate the second chance you are giving me and I'll spend the rest of my life trying to make this up to you and our family. I love you. Please stick with me.*
- **Grade B:** *I should never have had this affair. I started and then I couldn't stop. Soon I felt I was in so deep that I didn't know how to tell you. Every time I thought of telling you, I saw your face and couldn't do it. You and the kids mean more to me. I am sorry. It won't happen again.*

- **Grade C:** *I am sorry for this. I don't know why I did this and I'll never do it again. Let's put this behind us and go on with our lives. I'll do better. I love you and the kids.*
- **Grade F:** *Okay, Kiddo. It's over now. Let's go out and celebrate. I was a bad boy. I'll do better.*

In some cases, it may be appropriate for him to apologize to your parents. A therapist can help him navigate this tricky situation. If verbalizing is not appropriate, something special, like his taking the family to a special dinner, an evening out, or on a long weekend vacation may be a **symbolic apology,** with little said about the past and more about the future. This way parents, siblings, and children can understand that a healing has begun, and will continue to take place.

Reparations

Another step in healing is reparations, which means your partner gives you a gift to help you in your recovery and as a way to symbolically "pay" for your pain. I ask those clients I work with to think of something appropriate. Some retake their vows, some go on a trip, and some purchase an appropriate gift. Many seem to like buying something for their home, such as artwork, while others buy a piece of jewelry for the wife. This gift marks the end of a bad period and the beginning of something new.

Make an Agreement

The last step is to make an agreement with each other. You can write the agreement together. One man wrote a Bill of Rights for his wife. Whatever you call it, the agreement helps him promise to not be unfaithful, to be tuned in to stress, to share with you any attraction to anyone of the opposite sex, and most important, to talk to the other one about your concerns. This agreement can be written or verbalized. What is most important is that you both understand it and agree to it.

An agreement can be something like this:

I promise not to have an affair and not to keep any secrets from you. I will share any problems or concerns with you so that we can use effective communication to work on solving those problems. If someone comes on to me anywhere, I will not respond or encourage it. I will tell you about it. I will not keep secrets or keep anything from you again. If I become attracted to another person anywhere, I promise to tell you as soon as I recognize it.

I will not keep secrets. I will not lie to you. I will not deceive you. I will answer any questions honestly. I will talk about this at our private Talk Time.

I will honor our vows.

Man's signature
Woman's signature
Date

Will He Cheat Again?

No one has a crystal ball to tell the future, but you can look for some positive indicators that lead you to believe he won't cheat again. If the following things are true, he is unlikely to cheat again:

1. He never had an affair before this.
2. His friends have not had affairs.
3. He is remorseful.
4. He has done everything he could to help you heal.
5. He has ended the affair.
6. He has not seen her again.
7. He understands and accepts the causes for the affair.
8. He has made changes so that the causes are no longer there.
9. He promises never to have an affair again.
10. He keeps his promises.
11. He has been respectful to your parents through this.
12. You have reached an agreement with each other about affairs.
13. You have family meetings and personal meetings.

14. You remember to nurture your marriage with dates, fun get-aways, and flirtations.

These are the signs that things are changing for the better. If you can say "yes" to all of these, you are doing well (he must be able to say "yes" to the first ten). If not, you have more work to do.

This book was written so that the underlying causes for affairs can be looked at on a continuum, starting at one end with those that can have the best outcome, along the continuum to those where it is more difficult to expect a positive outcome. You can judge at what point the affair falls, and make your assessment from that.

YOU MUST KNOW WHY

To try to make the marriage affair-proof, the reason for the affair must be identified, so that the appropriate course of therapy is prescribed. It is important that both understand it and agree to it.

We have taken this journey together and reviewed many painful events along the way. I leave you with suggestions for strengthening your marriage and making it a fortress from the cold and ruthless winds from without. You are fortified, you are stronger, and you have the will to continue building the most effective and comforting relationship you can create. Much good luck.

Afterword:
How to Be a Survivor

Step 1: Heal

After first discovering the affair, you should concentrate on healing yourself from the pain of the aftermath, the blow to your sense of self, your self-esteem, and your trust. You should put all your efforts into gathering your support, finding a therapeutic network, and nurturing yourself, using all of the skills taught in this book to help you.

Step 2: Gather Information

As you begin to hear the story of his infidelity, try to understand what happened and why. Review each other's background, family and life events, the world you live in, your belief systems, your goals, your hopes and disappointments. Answer the questions at the end of each chapter, to try to find understanding as well as the answer for the ending you want for yourselves.

Step 3: Restructure Your Life

With this understanding, make choices for your story: what you want to happen, what changes need to be made, and how to make them happen, taking into consideration the needs of your children and family and how they will be met. You both need to search for the answers from a similar understanding and common goals.

Step 4: Make It Happen

Both partners must share in making your story have a satisfactory ending—that is, by having complete participation in Talk Time, family meetings, and honest communication—*devoting two years to the change.* Then a reconfiguration of behaviors will start to happen. Communication will be honest, treatment of everyone involved will be respectful, and family life can become enjoyable. You will become stronger than you ever believed possible from having gone through this transition and discovering new skills and strength. At the end of that time you will be a survivor.

Being a Survivor

When my coauthor, Gloria G. Harris, and I wrote *Surviving Infidelity*, we described in detail our view of what it takes to be a survivor. Here is the list we compiled. These thoughts continue to be a beacon to anyone surviving a difficult situation.

- Believe in your own resourcefulness
- Withstand uncomfortable feelings
- Believe in something greater than yourself
- See the complexity of events
- View events in a time frame
- Formulate a plan
- Ask for help and support
- Let go of resentment
- Recognize the power of thoughts for healing
- Find meaning in one's experience

That last point is a very important one: searching for meaning. The final step is integrating this experience into your life—that is, having it become part of your history rather than an ongoing obsession.

Realize the power you have **to change your life** and, perhaps, **those of people you meet along the way!**

Most efforts can be modest, but still enormously helpful. For example, some who suffered from the effects of infidelity have become peer counselors for women who have experienced the same thing. Others have donated books on the topic to the local library.

Not everyone who has experienced infidelity wants to go public with it, but I know one woman who did, and she has helped thousands of couples. Peggy Vaughan has worked through the pain that she and her husband, James, experienced because of his infidelity.

Peggy then started a national support group called BAN (Beyond Affairs Network) and the websites *www.preventingaffairs.com* and *www.dearpeggy.com*, which help people and educate them about infidelity. At this point, you may not be able to see that far, but it is possible to pass lessons on and become a beacon of light to others along the way. By making the effort, you will grow and those around you will rejoice in the change, and join you in your belief in your future.

Although we need to understand our past, and we must plan for our future, we should be mindful of our present. We must live in the moment, taking one day at a time, one moment at a time, appreciating the good we come across, and trying to change that which calls out for help.

Good luck and good wishes.

Appendix A:
Self-Assessment

Now that you have finished the book, answer these questions to help you assess your partner's affair. This is a private and personal assessment designed to help you apply what you have read to your life.

Overview

1. How would you categorize your husband's affair? The infidelity was a:

   Serial Affair: Yes/No

   Fling: Yes/No

   Romantic Love Affair: Yes/No

   Long-Term Affair: Yes/No

   Emotional Affair: Yes/No

   Cyber Affair: Yes/No

   If "Yes," do you think it is:

   a. A true cyber affair: Yes/No

   b. An addiction: Yes/No

   If you suspect addiction, have you seen a therapist so that therapy can get started? Yes/No

   (If not, remember that you can go alone for therapy.)

2. Has he ended the affair? Yes/No

   If "No," why hasn't he ended the affair?

Communication

1. Are you having family meetings? Yes/No
2. Are you scheduling Talk Time? Yes/No
3. Are you using the "I" message? Yes/No
4. Are you using empathy when you reply? Yes/No
5. Have you reduced the number of "harsh start-ups"? Yes/No
6. Are you listening carefully? Yes/No
7. Have you refrained from denying each other's experience? Yes/No
8. Have you stopped talking over the other person? Yes/No
9. Have you refrained from interrupting? Yes/No
10. Have you refrained from using sarcasm? Yes/No
11. Do you remember to use time-outs when necessary? Yes/No
12. Do you notice an improvement in your communication? Yes/No
13. Are you able to talk about issues politely and make progress in your Talk Time sessions? Yes/No
14. Are you able to use family meetings to plan activities with the family? Yes/No

If you have answered "Yes" to most of these questions, your communication sounds as though it is doing well.

15. How would your husband answer the same questions?

Health/Lifestyle

1. Have you or any member of your family had a troubling health problem in the two years before the affair? Yes/No
2. Have you been coping with an ongoing problem, that is, a chronic health condition, poverty, or situation that is not likely to change? Yes/No
3. Has your home been chaotic or disorganized? Yes/No
4. Do the members of the family speak politely to each other? Yes/No

5. Do you consider your home "hostile territory"? Yes/No
6. Do your husband and you find time for sex? Yes/No
7. Is sex enjoyable for both of you? Yes/No
8. Do you feel stressed from the geographical separation you and your husband are experiencing? Yes/No/NA
9. Has there been bereavement in your family that is constantly on your mind? Yes/No
10. Have you lost interest in sex? Yes/No
11. Has your husband lost interest in sex? Yes/No
12. Do you have in-law problems? Yes/No
13. Are you negatively affected in attitude by getting older? Yes/No
14. Is your husband negatively affected in attitude by either of you getting older? Yes/No
15. I worry that my husband could be described as
    The Macho Man: Yes/No
    The Power Man: Yes/No
    The Controlling Man: Yes/No
    The Narcissistic Man: Yes/No
    The Unstable, Moody Person: Yes/No
    The Sex Addict: Yes/No
    Spending an unusual amount of time on the computer: Yes/No

Contributors
1. I feel some of the contributors toward our problems are:
2. I feel that I have contributed to the general tone of the problems by: Not understanding/Not talking
3. Other:

Self-Help Plan

1. My plan for the future is:
2. My assets are:
   - ❏ Family:
   - ❏ Friends:
   - ❏ My faith:
   - ❏ Exercise:
   - ❏ Neighbors:
   - ❏ Support group:
   - ❏ Therapist:
   - ❏ Work:
   - ❏ Organizations I belong to:
   - ❏ My hobbies:
   - ❏ My interests:
   - ❏ My home:
   - ❏ Financial:
   - ❏ Other:

Appendix B:
8 Infidelity Myths Debunked

1. The affairee is more beautiful than the partner.
Usually, she isn't. Many reports say that she is not as pretty as the partner.

2. If he cheats once, he will cheat again.
This applies for the men further along the continuum—serial lovers, macho men, and those with psychological and personality problems. A man who has one or two flings may never cheat again. The answer is to find out why he cheated and attend to those issues.

3. A little flirting won't do any harm.
Yes, it could. The first stage of an affair starts with flirting, and it sends a message that says, "I am interested." This is crossing a boundary.

4. It is okay for my husband, who has had an affair, to contact an old flame.
It is dangerous to your marriage for your partner to contact an old flame. If she is visiting and wants to see him, be sure you go together and that this is the end of their contact.

5. The affairee is a better sex partner.
Usually, the reports are that the sex is better at home. The affairee offers a "bubble" environment, free from stress.

6. If you can't forgive him, you will have no future together.

If you can't forgive, it doesn't mean you don't have a future together. You must be able to understand why he had the affair and to make the necessary changes for the happiness and well-being of you both.

7. If children don't know, it can't hurt them.

Children may not know that their father had an affair, but they will know that something is wrong in the home. It is impossible to hide the tensions from children, and when the father sees the hurt, disappointment, and anger children can feel about his being unfaithful to their mother, he may be very remorseful. Caution: Do not use children as an ally, because it will harm them.

8. Most affairs end with the cheating spouse leaving the marriage for the affairee.

Studies show that fewer than 10 percent leave the marriage for the other person.

Bibliography

Botwin, Carol. *Men Who Can't Be Faithful*. New York: Warner Books, 1988.

Bowen, Murray. *Family Therapy in Clinical Practice*. New York: Jason Aaronson, 1978.

Burns, David. *Feeling Good*. New York: William Morrow and Company, 1989.

Carnes, Patrick. *Out of the Shadows*. Minneapolis: CompCare, 1992.

Cooper, Alvin, *Cybersex and Sexual Compulsivity: The Dark Side of the Force*. New York: Brunner/Mazel, 2000.

Edwards, Elizabeth. *Resilience*. New York: Broadway Books, 2009.

Elliott, Timothy. "Counseling Adults from Schlossberg's Adaptation Model." *American Mental Health Counselors Association Journal* 7 (July 1985).

Ellis, Albert, and Robert A. Harper. *A New Guide to Rational Living*. North Hollywood, CA: Wilshire Books, 1975.

Erikson, Erik. *Childhood and Society*. New York: W.W. Norton, 1950.

Frankl, Viktor E. *Man's Search for Meaning*. Boston: Beacon Press, 1963.

Gilligan, Carol. *In a Different Voice*. Cambridge, MA: Harvard University Press, 1982.

Glass, Shirley. *Not "Just Friends": Protect Your Relationship from Infidelity and Heal the Trauma of Betrayal*. New York: Free Press, 2003.

Gottman, John M., and Nan Silver. *The Seven Principles for Making Marriage Work*. New York: Crown, 1999.

Hotchkiss, Sandy. *Why Is It Always About You?* New York: Free Press, 2002.

Kalish, Nancy. *Lost and Found Lovers: Facts and Fantasies of Rekindled Romances*. New York: Morrow, 1997.

Lawson, Annette. *Adultery*. New York: Basic Books, 1988.

Layton-Tholl, D. "Extramarital Affairs: The Link Between Thought Suppression and Level of Arousal." Abstract in *Dissertation Abstracts International, Section B: The Sciences and Engineering* (1999): 2348.

Maheu, Marlene, and Rona Subotnik. *Infidelity on the Internet: Virtual Relationships and Real Betrayal*. Naperville, IL: Sourcebooks, 2001.

Marcus, Irwin M. *Why Men Have Affairs*. New Orleans, LA: Bon Temps Press, 2004.

Maltz, Maxwell. *Psycho-Cybernetics: A New Way to Get More Living Out of Life*. New York: Pocket Books, 1967.

McGoldrick, Monica, and Randy Gerson. *Genograms in Family Assessment*. New York: W.W. Norton, 1985.

Michael, Robert T., John H. Gagnon, Edward O. Laumann, and Gina Kolata. *Sex in America: A Definitive Survey.* New York: Warner Books, 1995.

Pittman, Frank. *Man Enough.* New York: G.P. Putnam's Sons, 1993.

Reinisch, June. *The Kinsey Institute New Report on Sex.* New York: St. Martin's Press, 1990.

Roth, Kimberlee, and Freda B. Friedman. *Surviving a Borderline Parent.* Oakland, CA: New Harbinger, 2003.

Sager, Clifford. *Marriage Contracts and Couple Therapy.* New York: Brunner/Mazel, 1976.

Schlossberg, Nancy. "A Model for Analyzing Human Adaptation to Transitions." *Counseling Psychologist* 9(2): 2–18.

———. *Counseling Adults in Transition.* New York: Springer, 1984.

Schneider, Jennifer. "Effects of Cybersex Addiction on the Family: Results of a Survey." In *Cybersex: The Dark Side of the Force,* edited by Alvin Cooper, 31–58. New York: Brunner/Mazel, 2000.

Sternberg, Robert. *The Triangle of Love: Intimacy, Passion, Commitment.* New York: Basic Books, 1988.

Subotnik, Rona. "Cyber Infidelity." In *Infidelity: A Practitioner's Guide to Working with Couples in Crisis,* edited by Paul R. Peluso, 169–190. New York: Routledge, 2007.

———. *Will He Really Leave Her for Me?* Avon, MA: Adams Media, 2005.

Subotnik, Rona, and Gloria Harris. *Surviving Infidelity: Making Decisions, Recovering from the Pain.* 3rd ed. Avon, MA: Adams Media, 2005.

Trotter, R. J. "The Three Faces of Love." *Psychology Today* (September 1986): 47–54.

Vaughan, Peggy. (1989). *The Monogamy Myth: A New Understanding of Affairs and How to Survive Them.* New York: NewMarket Press, 1989.

Weiss, Robert. "When Sex Is the Drug." *The Therapist* 19(1): 73–80.

Woo, Stephanie, and Carolyn Keatinge. "Personality Disorders." In *Diagnosis and Treatment of Mental Disorders Across the Life Span,* 801–877. Hoboken, NJ: Wiley, 2008.

Index

when he "doesn't know why," 50, 51

when it "meant nothing," 50

Relaxation techniques, 179

Religion, apologies and, 167

Reparations, 205

Retaliation affairs, 117–19

Romantic love affairs, 8, 10–12, 15, 22. *See also* Emotional affairs

Secret lives, 13, 16

Serial affairs, 6–8, 9, 12, 132, 135–37, 158, 167–68

Sex. *See* Intimacy

Sexual addiction, 157–60. *See also* Serial affairs

  case study, 159–60

  characteristics of, 157–58

  chemistry of, 157–58

  dealing with, 158–59

  Internet and, 32–33

  legacy of, 78

  macho men vs. addicts, 132–33

  understanding, 30

Specialness, losing, 169

Stages of affairs, 14–16

Stress

  change/transitions and, 60, 61–62, 63–64, 65–66, 71

  commitment/expectations and, 41, 42, 43, 45

  identifying and managing, 47, 55, 65–66

  leading to affairs, 42, 43, 45, 60, 94, 104

  non-events and, 61

  ongoing, 63–64

  questions to assess, 55

Support. *See also* Cognitive therapy; Coping skills; *specific affair type*

  professional help, 196–97

  for sexual addiction, 158–59

  transitions and, 64–65

Surviving infidelity, guidelines, 209–11

Suspicions, confronting him about, 17–18

Talk time, 176–77

Thinking

  distortions in, 181–86, 187

  rational, 186–87, 188

  rationalization and, 81–82, 188–89

Timing of affairs, 17

Transitions, 59–74

  about: overview of, 60

  case study of affair from, 65–73

  defined, 60

  expected ("on-time"), 60

  hope for affairs caused by, 64–65

  how affairs arise from, 66

  non-event, 61

  off-time, 62–63

  ongoing stresses and, 63–64

  questions to ask about, 74

  support systems and, 64–65

  unexpected, 61–62

  working through affair from, 69–70

Trust

  emotional abandonment and, 169

  intimacy and, 40–41

  rebuilding, 203. *See also* Cognitive therapy

Unavailable partner, affairs and, 103–6

Unfulfilled expectations, 112–17

Woods, Tiger, 138

Writing

  by him, to document thoughts, 202

  by you, to relieve anger, 180–81

About the Author

RONA B. SUBOTNIK is a licensed marriage and family therapist. She is the coauthor of one of the bestselling books on infidelity, *Surviving Infidelity: Making Decisions, Recovering from the Pain*, published in 1994 and updated in its second edition in 1999 and third edition in 2005. She is also the coauthor of *Infidelity on the Internet: Virtual Relationships and Real Betrayal*, published in 2001. In addition, she is the author of *Will He Really Leave Her for Me?* This was the first self-help book of its kind, published in 2005. She has appeared on the *Leeza Show* on national television, and on Canadian radio, Radio Free Europe, and Voice of America discussing infidelity. She has been interviewed for major newspapers and magazines, such as the *Chicago Tribune*, *San Diego Union Tribune*, *Palm Springs Desert Sun*, and *Newsweek*.

Mrs. Subotnik has been in private practice for eighteen years in California. She is married and has three adult children. She lives in Palm Desert, where she is in private practice.

You can reach Mrs. Subotnik through her website at *www.survive infidelity.com* or *www.ronasubotnik.com*.